BLIND

Not

BROKEN

BLIND
Not
BROKEN

Your guide to turning loss
and grief into happiness

LUCY EDWARDS

hamlyn

hamlyn

First published in Great Britain in 2024 by Hamlyn, an imprint of
Octopus Publishing Group Ltd
Carmelite House
50 Victoria Embankment
London EC4Y 0DZ
www.octopusbooks.co.uk

An Hachette UK Company
www.hachette.co.uk

Distributed in the US by
Hachette Book Group
1290 Avenue of the Americas
4th and 5th Floors
New York, NY 10104

Distributed in Canada by
Canadian Manda Group
664 Annette St.
Toronto, Ontario, Canada M6S 2C8

ISBN 978-0-600-63765-3

A CIP catalogue record for this book is available from the British Library.

Typeset in 12.5/18.5pt Sabon LT Pro by Jouve (UK), Milton Keynes.

Printed and bound in Great Britain.

1 3 5 7 9 10 8 6 4 2

Publishers: Eleanor Maxfield and Natalie Bradley
Editor: Sarah Allen
Design Director: Mel Four
Production Manager: Caroline Alberti

This FSC® label means that materials used
for the product have been responsibly sourced.

CONTENTS

Introduction: A Bit of Hair and a Whole
Lot to Share   1

1   Childhood/Early Life: Before Sight Loss   19
2   Shock and Denial
    (THE FIRST STAGE OF GRIEF)   39
3   The Early Days: Pain and Guilt
    (THE SECOND STAGE OF GRIEF)   71
4   Anger and Bargaining
    (THE THIRD STAGE OF GRIEF)   91
5   Loneliness and Depression
    (THE FOURTH STAGE OF GRIEF)   113
6   The Upward Turn: Communication
    and Relationships
    (THE FIFTH STAGE OF GRIEF)   133
7   Starting to Think of Myself Differently:
    Confidence and Identity Reconstruction
    (THE SIXTH STAGE OF GRIEF)   169
8   Bats Aren't Disabled: Acceptance
    (THE SEVENTH STAGE OF GRIEF)   193

Epilogue: How does a Blind Girl…?   211
Acknowledgements   231
Endnotes   234

INTRODUCTION:
A BIT OF HAIR AND
A WHOLE LOT TO SHARE

The last room I ever saw was the inpatient ward at Moorfields Eye Hospital.

On 23 March 2013 at 8am I was sitting in my hospital gown and very glamorous knee-high, bright-white hospital socks. An arrow was drawn just above my left eyebrow in marker pen, pointing down to be sure the correct eye would be operated on. I didn't want to believe I was losing my eyesight, but, as the hours ticked by, I longed for my name to be called to head into the operating theatre. I wished with every atom of my being that I could be on that plane with my friends right now. They were off on a history A-level trip to Poland that I should have been on. I unlocked my iPhone and scrolled to my Spotify playlist called 'Bye Eye'. Shaking, I plugged in my headphones and listened to 'Echo' by songwriters Jason Walker and Nicholle Anne Galyon. To this day, I find it hard to listen to that song without thinking about what happened. I remember repeating the lyrics 'I don't really know where the world is but I miss it now'. I felt numb and in a trance.

My mum, Auntie Kaz and I had arrived at the hospital early. We were informed that I would be the first operation of the day, but I ended up being the last. At around mid-afternoon my consultant, whom I had known since I lost sight in my right eye, came to see me and my family. It just so happened that he was retiring in the same week when I was losing everything. I couldn't help but take that as a little sign from the universe. He had cared for me for over six years and I had always respected and valued him, so I felt really touched that he had come to see me.

He looked at me and said, 'Lucy we always hoped it wouldn't come to this.'

Mum and Kaz never stopped holding my hands and kissing my face. The consultant walked away and I started crying.

It was like time stopped – in one instant I had hope for my future, and then that hope was swallowed by a black hole. I started to really evaluate what hope now meant for me because, as he said the word 'hope', the more I believed there wasn't any left. If the doctors who had been taking care of me for so many years didn't know how to cure my blindness, then what was this 'hope' that I had been believing and investing in for almost ten years? What was hope when I had been waiting for my eyes to get better and they weren't going to? What was hope when I had spent hours and hours at hospital appointments only to lose hope?

So much expectation, so much desire for a sighted future, but it all seemed so futile as I realized I had no control over my own body anymore. Hoping my eyes would work one day was never going to actually make them work!

I had always been told by medical professionals that they weren't sure what my eyes would do, but, because I was functioning day to day, I wanted to believe that I would have sight forever.

Kaz turned to me and said, 'This is not the end of Lucy Edwards.' Her words are moulded into my memory because I didn't believe her – I felt that it *was* the end of me. I could have never imagined what my life now would be and how the smallest of changes could make the biggest of differences.

If you had said to me back then, 'Luce, you're going to be the face of a global haircare brand', I would have spat out my drink, got back into bed and refused to believe you. But, in 2021, I found myself sitting in front of the Pantene team, the production crew, lights, cameras and one of the best directors in the world – Paola Kudacki; I told myself how proud I was to be living in this moment. I didn't care about the 12-hour shoot days, the hot lamps or the number of times I had to get changed, because eight years previously I had lost my vision, my childhood and my mind. I had goosebumps.

I sat in the backstage loo with my hair in rollers having flashbacks to the moments when I told myself that I couldn't go on anymore, holding back happy tears, thankful that I never gave up.

'So how many people are there, Ali?' I asked.

'Loads Lu; there must be about 100 people in the studio – it's massive, probably about five times the size of Mum and Dad's kitchen. All of the walls and ceiling are white and there are so many people running around with different equipment, cameras, microphones, a sound desk. There are two giant umbrella-shaped lights beaming on to a white wall, wooden laminate, a seat and a desk where you're going to be sitting!'

My sister held out my Spanx underwear while in the loo with me helping me step into them.

'What's the colour of the buttons on my dress? Do they match the dress nicely?'

'They are rounded in shape and covered in the same satin material as the dress, Lucy.'

Alice helped me do up the buttons on my silky dress so that my nails, which had been painted specially, wouldn't be damaged.

We walked out of the bathroom into my dressing room and Alice instinctively described what everything looked like, as she always did:

'We are in the make-up room, Lu. All the make-up and hair tools are laid out beautifully on the table, with a few large hairdressing chairs, and a massive rectangular mirror with large-bulb beauty lights around it. The room is very, very narrow.'

As the hairdresser took my rollers out, I turned to Alice and asked her excitedly, 'What's my hair look like now with the rollers out?'

'It looks like Hollywood hair – massive, sculpted

waves, shiny and copper in colour. You look gorgeous –
you remind me of Marilyn Monroe.'

We chatted as Alice took behind-the-scenes video
footage for my social media channels.

I love Alice's audio description over anyone else's –
she is my mirror. I can always rely on her to be clear
and direct. She puts me at ease and makes me laugh
all at the same time. I remember her calling me 'Angel
drawers' as my make-up was glowing and I wore a
satin cream dress – there's nothing quite like your sister
bringing you back down to Earth.

My new make-up artist, Eloise, had just applied my
eyeliner – something I had never had done before. Up
until this point, either me or my sister had always done
my make-up. I felt anxious every time I went to look for
a make-up artist. As a blind person, I only ever trusted
Alice with my face so I had never hired someone to do
my make-up. It felt lovely to get it done, but also very
odd because I couldn't necessarily have an opinion
on how I looked when it was complete, and because I
hadn't made the brush strokes or picked the product,
I felt detached from the experience somewhat. Usually
Alice and I would talk about every little stage and
detail if I wore new products so it felt less scary. This
was a different experience that I relaxed into after a few

hours. As I chatted to Eloise and she audio-described what she looked like, I became comfortable and felt like I had known her for years. It was refreshing that my work was allowing me to see another side of myself that I had never seen before. I was now relinquishing control of my look in order for Pantene to get the right shot, which tested me. I liked that a production team was handling everything. The only real way to determine how beautiful I feel is the ritual, the routine and the feeling. When those are stripped away, it is about the visuals, but there was a beauty in thinking about the words I was saying in more detail, not worrying about my make-up but connecting with my make-up artist and learning to trust new people. My appearance was something I had never let anyone else comment on other than Alice, Mum and Kaz for eight years throughout my whole blindness journey because I felt vulnerable. There is a beauty in shaking things up a little and doing something new.

After so many hours of chatting to the crew, I felt at home. I met so many lovely like-minded people and had to pinch myself at the end of day one that this was now my job.

Trying on my silky cream button-down dress, there was some last-minute tailoring for the seamstress to do. I waited in my fluffy dressing gown for my outfit to be ready while I ate some breakfast. Every time I ate or drank anything, my dress would be taken to be steamed by the stylists. I was quite nervous and running on adrenaline, but after I had some photos taken and started to film some lines of my advert, I felt so happy in front of the camera. The nerves were replaced with excitement that I was doing a job I was born to do.

On day two, my brand-new guide dog – Molly – was on set so she could walk me up the street. She did so well as we had only been matched with each other for a month or so. We hadn't even qualified as a partnership yet, so my guide dog mobility specialist, Amanda, brought her to the set and helped me out with her. Her little crimped fluffy ears, her golden coat and her lovely calm temperament made the production team want to stroke her – who can blame them? – but the director on the microphone reminded everyone not to pet a working dog. I had been without a guide dog for eight months as my previous girl, Olga, had to retire. When I once again held my guide dog's harness, I felt free and able to express myself.

At the end of the shoot, the whole crew clapped me for my work. I was on cloud nine. My new manager,

Alan, handed me my Diet Coke and told me that that was the biggest clap he had ever heard on a shoot like this. I knew nothing about the world of social media and advertising, so having him to guide me was invaluable. Smiling from ear to ear, I practically skipped off the set.

Being chosen as Pantene's newest ambassador means that, after years of walking into Boots or Superdrug and every bottle feeling the same, things are going to change. Now, when I or any other visually-impaired (VI) person purchases a Pantene product, they will have all the information they need because Pantene have collaborated with an app company called NaviLens that allows you to find and locate information easily. You don't need to know where QR codes are placed; you can just scan the product with your phone's camera and get the necessary information. Every Pantene product will have a NaviLens code on it, meaning that when you scan around the shop shelves with your smartphone, it will read out every product name, the ingredients, the user instructions, the price and much more. Up until now, you had to have good aim or some vision to scan an ordinary barcode on, say, a tin of beans, but not anymore.

It's proof that the smallest changes can make the biggest difference – it means that, for the first time, not everything in this world is just about how something looks; it's about how it feels. It means that we are finally seeing disability representation in the mainstream where it belongs.

Every day I remind myself how lucky and grateful I am to be a spokesperson for blind people everywhere because, when I lost my sight, I didn't have anyone to look up to and I hated being different. I have embraced my sight loss and everything that this journey has taught me. Do I feel emotional that I am in such a position of power and a global brand has trusted me to represent them...? Of course! When you have just had your eye sewn back up and you are learning how to pour a drink again, it's not something that you think will ever genuinely happen.

When you are living through a life-altering illness, it's impossible to see a future, VI or not. Also, when you live in a sighted world for 17 years and suddenly everything you hold now isn't accessible, it's hard to think of a world that offers that freedom back again.

But why should you care about my journey?

Well, dear lovely reader, joy.

I want to share my sight loss story with you because,

even if our path to grief has been different, we can all relate in some way. I know what it's like to not want to live anymore, for your whole life to change in one instant, to no longer recognize yourself. But I also know what it is like to film a major TV advert, find love, have a successful career, be independent and live your dream life.

This is a book for anyone dealing with loss and grief. It's for anyone who can't see a happy tomorrow. It's for anyone who can't reconcile the person they are now with the person they used to be. It's a book for a parent, friend, family member or loved one of someone going through a life-altering, world-shattering, heartbreaking event.

It's a book for those who can't accept what has happened in their life and can't process it years later. It's for anyone who, like me, has missed out on life's big milestones because, while everyone else their age was thriving, they were doing their best to survive.

After reading my book, I hope you'll know that, just because life is hard at the moment and you are running 'behind' everyone else, it doesn't mean you can't forge your own path as I did.

Society says that you have to drive a car, go to university, get married at a certain age and live life in a certain order, but what happens to your plans and your mental health when a life-changing event means that order no longer applies to you? It took me a long time to figure out that I am the one writing the script for my own life, and I wanted to create a resource so you don't have to take as long to get back on your feet as I did.

Readjusting your path is scary and traumatic, especially because these milestones are what everyone expects of you, but remember that other people's expectations are not your reality. The only limits that we have are the ones we place on ourselves, because no one else has the right to comment. One person may get out and about using a mobility aid such as a wheelchair, a long white cane, a Zimmer frame, a motorized vehicle, a guide dog or a walking stick, but none of these modes of transport are any less valid than the other. They are just different. Just because we aren't the default 'normal' human does not mean that our lives are any less valid. What is normal anyway? The beauty of life is that we are all different otherwise it would be boring.

Just because one part of you has died doesn't mean you can't love this version of yourself; it is just going to take time. While you are taking things day by day, I want to give you tips, insight, positivity and practical solutions to feel happier with yourself, as well as hopefully make you laugh and smile along the way with my life story up till this point.

Use this book as a companion to get you through this hard time; a way for you to relax and unwind after a stressful day. Do the exercises included at the end of each chapter when you are having a self-care day and taking some time for yourself. We all need to make some space to just breathe and reflect on what has happened in our lives.

I hope to show you that, just because you are different now, does not mean you are broken. You just need to find that part of you that can sparkle again. Just like my guide dog Molly guides me, I will guide you to find a different but amazing version of yourself. Now, let's get started!

THE STAGES OF GRIEF

Anyone who has experienced grief will know that it is not something that ever really goes away, and it creeps up on you unexpectedly. My mum, who worked as a palliative care nurse, would occasionally talk about loss when I was a child if I was upset, and would explain a theory of loss to me in a child-friendly way. This theory, by Elisabeth Kübler-Ross, talks about stages of grief defined as denial, anger, bargaining, depression and acceptance. This model was introduced to help terminally ill patients confront their own death and though it was never intended to be used by people who would live with grief, I found her ideas loosely applied to my situation when chatting with my mum. They seemed to help me at the time, although I don't think the stages seem as clear as this when it's actually happening to you! It's only now, as I write this book, that I realize my experiences mirror some of these stages. The grief I experienced definitely isn't linear in this way and feels very 'all over the place'. Indeed, this was the main criticism of the model – that stages didn't happen in a linear way and that not all people experience all of the emotions detailed in the model. I have loosely explored seven stages of grief by mentioning them in the context of my journey below, but don't forget that it's a huge subject and to do it justice we would be reading for hours! These are just some of the things I felt, and the huge variations in theory (some talk of five stages or different types of grief) could be explored in a lot more detail. My reality was that I found it best not to set limits or a time frame on the grief process and know that everyone's different.

The first stage: Shock and denial

Generally understood as a period when we refuse to acknowledge or deny our loss, this may also include a period of numbness. I spent many years in denial of my sight loss and I would agree that this denial and shock provided emotional protection. In my case, this went on for many years.

The second stage: Pain and guilt

This is when the loss of love or any loss is felt and the pain of this starts to become very real and upsetting. You may feel guilty for needing more help from those around you – for me this was certainly a very big thing. It felt like an intense pain losing my eyesight and anyone who has lost something very dear to them will identify with the immediate hurt that this brings. It's worth remembering that what happens in these moments is etched in your memory.

The third stage: Anger and bargaining

When I think about feeling angry about my sight loss it's always the thing I feel most upset about, but it's worth noting that it's very natural to feel angry. It's also very normal to bargain with yourself. This is described by many theorists as the point at which we start to make deals with ourselves. I can remember the times when I felt angry at everyone and I thought that perhaps if I had managed something differently then I wouldn't be finding a situation so hard. This is a difficult time and having loved ones close who understand this is vital.

The fourth stage: Loneliness and depression

I really started to feel like I didn't want to bother doing things, slept for long periods and gave up on life for a long while when the reality of my sight loss becoming permanent kicked in – the loneliness and isolation of being non-sighted in a sighted world that made very few provisions for blind people. The times when I am having a bad blind day remind me that the grief process definitely isn't linear and how I have to be mindful and careful to look after my mental health.

The fifth and sixth stages:
Upward turn and reconstruction

For me, developing new meaning for life as non-sighted Lucy took time. Gradually, as the days moved on,

I started to work out how I might be able to adjust to a new life. One standout moment for me was deciding to wear only cream, black and white clothes on a daily basis because I didn't want to worry about wearing clashing colours and patterns. This was a signal to me that I was starting to return to a new state of normal where I am happy to organise my wardrobe in a different way. Clothes, fashion and style still are an important part of my life, but I am able to accept that my everyday outfits are more monochrome to save time and mental energy.

The seventh stage: Acceptance

This is described as the time when we are able to start to live our life again. As I sit on a Zoom call talking about the social model of disability and saying I am happy being blind, it's clear to me that acceptance has arrived. The excruciating pain has lifted, and life can be experienced again. This doesn't stop the sadness at times, but to be able to find joy in life is an amazing feeling. Drawing a line in the sand between sighted Lucy and non-sighted Lucy allowed me to acknowledge what has been and who I was and accept what's yet to come. It's a good place to be.

Your journey doesn't have to fit into these categories, but knowing what may be ahead, may be of help.

You can make your own model – maybe grab a pen and your notebook and take some time to think about how it might look for you...

Exercise: Have a think about where you are now

- How have you related to the stages of grief so far?
- Describe how each stage of grief has affected you.

You can come back to this exercise.

Exercise: Create mini enjoyable moments

List three small activities you can do to have mini enjoyable moments, so you can build up to a day that's happier. At the beginning, it was an achievement if I lit a candle or played a song and sang to it. What are your three activities?

1

CHILDHOOD/EARLY LIFE: BEFORE SIGHT LOSS

When I was little, I was that girl stealing her mum's hairbrush, aka 'microphone', and parting the living room curtains to reveal myself and my sister Alice in tie-dye tops, crimped hair and Claire's Accessories make-up, presenting a whole talent show that involved Alice and our Bratz dolls singing along to S Club 7. I have always loved to create and perform. My childhood was packed full of happy memories, but, when I lost my vision, I lost myself and forgot who little Lucy was. I didn't recognize her anymore. For a long time I didn't want to think about little sighted Lucy as she was happier than the current version of myself.

To tell you the truth, a lot of the descriptions of the scenery and visual parts of the stories I am about to recount are visual memories from Dad that we chatted about before I wrote this chapter. I have completely blanked out my memory, which is called dissociative amnesia. This is a very common theme throughout my teens and early twenties. Everything I am recounting to you obviously happened to me first-hand, but has had to be bolstered by memories of family and friends who are the closest to me and who were with me in these moments in order to build up a picture for you.

I look back on my childhood years with such fondness now. It has taken me a long time to process who I was back then compared with the Lucy I am today. Bringing my pre-trauma memories together with my post-trauma self has been really hard.

For the first eight or so years of my life, I lived on a long crescent in Pelsall, Walsall in Birmingham (in the West Midlands). The street was full of brand-new houses, but not much plant life. I lived with my mum, dad and sister, Alice, around 35 minutes away from my extended family in Sutton Coldfield. We also had two little tabby cats named Max and Bruno. They were brothers from the local cats' home and Bruno was darker in colouring and Max a little lighter. Back then, my mum would work into the early hours on the wards as a nurse at the local hospital while my sister and I were fast asleep in bed. My dad would be the one to get us ready for his mum Sonia's (aka Nan's) house for the day, before he went to work as an electrical engineer. We would all get into his old army-green Vauxhall Nova saloon, a boxy square car that he bought off my grandad. He used to call it 'the green machine'. This was the late 1990s and, for context, just to get across how uncool our car was even back then, someone drove into the back of him after he dropped me and Alice off at Nan's one morning on the way to work. The insurance company found that it was the other person's fault, but didn't want to pay out to fix the damage because that would cost more than the price of the car itself. My dad bought it back off the insurance company for a few hundred quid anyway as we were quite tight on cash. We didn't have lots of money, but we were happy.

A lot of my early years were spent with my nan and I have such fond memories of those times. Nothing was too much trouble for her. She adored me and Alice, and my cousins. Nan's toast was like no one else's – Warburtons white toasty bread with Hartley's raspberry jam that she took the lumps out of for us. We would sit with her watching daytime TV and colouring in Groovy Chick colouring books. Alice says that I used to make her colour within the lines as I felt passionate that we needed to keep our books neat and someday hang them on the wall. Nan and Grandad's garden was amazing, too. In the summer, they brought out the sandpit and paddling pool. They even bought multicoloured balls and made a ball pit for us. They then bought a double swing and concreted it into the ground on the grass. Me, my sister and my cousins thought this was the best thing ever.

Making cards was one of my favourite things to do. Nan bought us whiteboards because I loved scoring things after watching *Strictly Come Dancing*, so I would be the judge while Alice and I took it in turns to dance. I even made a Len Goodman judging paddle with a number 7 on it. I was so fascinated with TV, sitting for hours printing off submission forms for me and my friends to appear on *Dick and Dom in da Bungalow*. That never happened because no one wanted to go on it with me even though I filled out everyone's forms. I applied for so many CBBC shows until one day I got a call to say that I could appear on *The Nelly Nut Show*. This was a game show where you just heard my voice live on air and I was up against another little girl. Whoever shouted the loudest would win. I was a little upset when the other contestant won the Nelly Nut mug. This just made me more determined to apply for more shows, but life went on and I continued to build my bamzooki robot on my dad's computer in my spare time.

One day, Nan let me cut my art project with big-girl scissors. She turned away for one minute to get me a drink and I cut off my fringe. Nan was mortified as it was so out of character for me and she was so worried to tell Mum, but she did and, when Mum came to pick me up after work that day, she just laughed.

My dad's sister, my lovely Auntie Kaz, worked at the local hospital and, in the summer holidays, me, Nan and Alice would walk up the road to meet her on her lunch break and share some chips in the hospital cafe. After work, she dropped in for a cuppa most weekdays, chatted to Nan and hung out with us. We used to play this game with Kaz where she would wrap me or Alice or my cousins in Nan's tartan picnic blanket. She would hold one side and my nan would hold the other. She would sing 'a leg and a wing to see the king...one, two, three'. On 'three', after swinging me round, she would release the blanket and I would know to jump out.

When we got home from Nan's, my mum always read us a story. It was a massive part of my childhood sitting on my mum and dad's bed with my sister at night reading. Mum would read us all sorts. *If My*

Dog Could Drive...I remember he used to really like avocados. *Commotion in the Ocean* was a firm favourite as well as the Mr Men books. Mine and Alice's favourite was *Mr Noisy* because Mum used to do voices and say, 'I'D LIKE A LOAF OF BREAD' and giggle. Mum would look back at Alice and ask her what had just happened in the story, but Alice would never be able to reply because she was so interested in giving Mum a new hairstyle while she giggled. I was 'Miss Goody Two-Shoes' and could always tell Mum what part she had just read. Mum loved that Alice and I were so different, and she celebrated that.

Dad painted my little box room bright orange. I had an IKEA silver metal bunk bed, which I thought was the coolest thing in the whole world because it had a little desk underneath with a futon. Alice's room was directly across the little hall from mine and our rooms were the same size with exactly the same bed and Groovy Chick bedding. Whatever I had, Alice had 'the same but different', as we would always say. My bedroom overlooked the front of the house and, one day, Mum was mowing the lawn and came in to make a drink and a burglar stole the lawnmower off the drive. I decided to make a sign and stick it on my window that warned them away. It was a very direct note that got straight to the point with questionable spelling: 'No burgalerrrs allowed'. I'm sure that helped a lot! I think little Lucy just wanted to have justice and saw this as a way of making a stand. I have always been a stickler for rules. The one time I had five minutes of my golden time removed (free time on Friday afternoon playtime at primary school) I cried all the way home and stayed up a lot of the night and told myself I wouldn't chatter to my friends during lessons again.

Birthdays and Christmases were always a massive thing in our household. Kaz and Nan would turn up with gorgeous presents wrapped in matching paper, usually of our favourite doll or TV show at the time. Mum and Kaz would always coordinate, and I would be so excited to wake up at the crack of dawn to open presents from Mum and Dad before Kaz and Nan got to the door before school. Dad would always say to us, 'You can come into our room and wake us if your alarm clock says 6am.' I would watch the clock, and it always felt so slow. One year, my parents bought me some Motorola walkie-talkies – one red and one blue. My dad at this point worked from home as a technical author in his office room which doubled up as the spare bedroom. As I walked to school with Mum we tested out how far the walkie-talkies would stay connected.

It was about half a mile before we lost each other. Dad always got us one tech present every year.

He bought and built us our first-ever desktop computers for our new rooms when we moved house to be nearer to my extended family when I was nine. We now only lived less than a five-minute walk to Nan's house and about an eight-minute walk to Kaz and her partner's (my uncle Nic) house. Dad is fab at DIY. As I mentioned previously, he is a qualified electrical engineer, but, in his apprentice years, he had experienced plumbing and general decorating skills. Dad prioritized decorating mine and Alice's rooms first. In order to make the rooms the same size, he knocked out the wall between the two rooms and built a wardrobe between the two. This made a little of Alice's wardrobe come into my room and Dad measured it exactly so the two rooms were the same. Dad made sure I had what I needed and, as my vision got worse, my desktop screen became a 32-inch TV with a cursor the size of my hand.

I had been diagnosed with my eyesight condition called incontinentia pigmenti at the age of eight after attending a routine eye exam at my local Specsavers. My family and I knew that my vision was a little worse than the average person's my age, but I still had two working eyes that were stable as far as we knew. I had always had black floaters that followed my vision around and I didn't notice the darkness getting bigger in the one eye because I thought everything was normal.

Two years later, that changed. It was 3.30pm on a lovely summer's day on an average Saturday in June 2006. The sun was shining brightly through the trees and ten-year-old me was at the last two miles of an eleven-mile-long cycle ride with my sister and parents. The Tissington Trail was around an hour's drive from where we lived and was a common route for families and long-distance cyclists to ride. I can't recall how long the track goes for, but young me really enjoyed stopping off at the various picnic benches and ice cream stalls along the way. We were only little – Alice was only nine at the time – and at points we would be tired so Mum would sit with us eating her family-famous egg mayo sandwiches while my dad did a few more miles and met us back at the bench. I remember when Mum and Dad bought us our bikes for Christmas in 2005. They were wrapped up in masses of wrapping paper. Alice and I had identical 20-inch-wheel, light-blue, Hotrock Specialized bikes with purple flowers on, and a white seat and handlebars. This summer was the very first one with our new bikes and I remember being so happy to get out with the wind in my hair.

On the way back, we all decided to go through a little old town on the route named Ashbourne. I remember riding along the slight slope downhill, so I didn't have to peddle that much to get to relatively high speeds, as I cranked down the gears. We came to a disused railway line under a tunnel. Underfoot there was lots of broken tarmac where the railway lines used to be that had obviously been dug up. The jagged road stones must have been as big as your hand. I was in front at the time, but the tunnel seemed unusually dark, so I shouted for my dad. He cycled as fast as he could to get ahead of me, but he didn't get to me in time. My front bike wheel had already lodged itself into a big stone as I fell over my handlebars and onto the ground. I remember crying quite hysterically on the floor, not only because I had quite a few gashes in my legs, but because I was frustrated that there were no lights in the tunnel. My mum and dad picked me up off the floor and gave me a kiss. I remember Dad turning to me and saying how sorry he was that he didn't realize it was too dark for me. I remember thinking, 'Why is he sorry? It's not his fault.' One moment I saw the floor before the tunnel and, in one flash, I couldn't see anymore. The incident went by so quickly that my ten-year-old brain couldn't process why I fell off my bike and everyone else could see the floor.

As we drove home in my dad's black Volvo after placing my new now-slightly-scratched bike on the roof rack, I started to wonder 'Why me?'. Why did I have to be the one to fall off my new bike? Didn't everyone else think it was really dark? In that moment I realized for the first time that I could no longer see in the dark. Coming to this realization at ten years old is scary beyond words because you are not able to process the enormity of what it truly means. Up until this point, for the last few years, my eyesight had been just something my parents and the consultants chatted about and I got my favourite dinner when I got home, but now I started to realize that maybe something might be actually really wrong. I didn't ride my bike much after this. I felt so scared that I would lose control of it and, if I am really truthful, I think I was blaming the bike for my fall because I couldn't truly believe that I was losing my eyesight. I couldn't really bring myself to believe that it happened even though it did. Writing this down it sounds so silly, but I didn't want it to be true.

I found myself making excuses about why I didn't have to go on my bike anymore, while also fighting with myself to build up the courage to do it again. My bike gathered dust in the garage because I was too scared. That one moment when I was ten years old shaped my future. I didn't know it yet, but that was just the first time out of many that my body gave up on me. When you are young you feel invincible, like your bones are spongey and life has no limits, but I learned at the age of ten that life does, in fact, have lots and lots of limits.

For a while after my sight loss, I used to bully myself in my mind. I would say that I am simply not good enough as this version of myself now I am blind. I used to think that all the experiences I had as a sighted kid were ruined because I now knew how evil the world could be. I knew that living a blind reality was harder and I used to resent the old version of me who had it easy, who sailed through life not thinking about how to access the materials at school, how to go out with friends or even walk anywhere new. I missed the freedom I once had and felt like I didn't harness or truly acknowledge what I had at the time.

I hated my past self so much, and ultimately this meant that I was consumed with this hateful feeling that was damaging the me who was living right now. Drowning in my own tears, I wondered if I would ever know who I was again.

I was constantly striving for old Lucy's happiness when I had no way to feel that particular moment of glee again. I was never going to live seven-year-old sighted Lucy's birthday again. I was never going to see my old bedroom or hold my old walkie-talkie again.

I was talking to my lovely dad one day and he said, 'You know, Lucy, as an older person, when I play a game that I used to as a child or watch a TV show that I used to love, it's somehow not the same now I am older. Sometimes it's good to leave lovely memories with your childhood nostalgia in your mind and think back to them and be glad they happened, not sad they are over.'

This really stuck with me. Sighted or not, we can all never go back. Life keeps on going. There is a beauty and a sadness in that, but it's beautifully sad. It's what makes memories so special and life worth living. So, I came to the conclusion that I needed to find a different happiness – one that I am happy with now.

This meant redefining what happiness meant to me as 20-something Lucy. I was blaming a lot of these bad feelings on my blindness, but some of what I was experiencing was just growing older, and some of it was grief. That grief cannot be understated. I don't believe that my grief will ever leave me. I don't want it to, because, if it did, I would have to forget about little sighted me and that erases a part of who I am. Even though it's painful sometimes to bring her along with the new me, I wouldn't be happy blind Lucy without her.

LOOKING BACK

It is okay to be sad about something you thought you had healed from. I used to think about events that happened in my life very separately. I would store them all away in my mind in different metaphorical filing cabinets. I would lock away the trauma or the life event in the cabinet, using two locks if I felt sick remembering the event, and move on with life.

I finally made peace with my past when I started to feel happy again. Something to say about happiness right off the bat is that no one on Earth is happy all the time. Others may give off the impression that they are, but this simply isn't realistic. Without sad moments you don't appreciate the happy memories.

Over time, I wanted to open the filing cabinets,

but it was too painful. I could never get rid of those memories even though I tried to lock them away forever as self-preservation. However, I realized that, without acknowledging the lows in life, I would not be prepared for the next inevitable challenge that life throws at me. I started to be glad that I had all these filing cabinets of experience to fall back on – it was useful to have them to open up and, eventually, I was glad to face my past...no matter how sad. This painful bit of self-acceptance enabled me to start thinking about my childhood again. Eventually, I realized that, as other hurdles arose, I was more equipped to deal with them having faced the past in this way.

As I became more compassionate for little sighted Lucy, I started to understand that I didn't need to compare myself to her. Her struggles were all relative and, if you let hate consume you, it really will. So really what I mean is that it's okay to still be sad about what you have lost and it's healthy to look back at the pages within your own filing cabinet from time to time. But, as you get to know yourself more, as time passes and you get further away from the trauma or event, you can definitely put it into perspective more and learn to live with your pain.

Happiness means something different to me now.

What does it mean for you? If you are reading this and don't feel ready for happiness to knock on your door, then you need some more time. Only you will know when that initial cloud of grief has passed. You probably have some heavy storms to weather yet, but, with time, you won't be rained on quite as much as you used to be. At first, you will have a blackout of any memories before the trauma and this is a part of your process to happiness again. It might take years and this is okay. It took me eight or nine years to smile about my lovely childhood again. In one way, this is sad, but it hasn't gone anywhere.

Resources

Looking back can be hard, but don't forget that professional support is always available to you. I still even have a regular counsellor now and I am not afraid to admit that. Even when I am in a good spot in my life, I always have one so I am checking in with myself all of the time. Organizations like the ones below can be helpful:

Samaritans: www.samaritans.org

Mind: www.mind.org.uk

WHAT DOES HAPPINESS MEAN FOR ME?

On the following page are some quick exercises that I like to do to sit with my thoughts when I am feeling a bit low. When people talked about meditation, I always used to think that it wouldn't really work for me. But the more I did these exercises and the more I built them into my regular routine, the more effective they became. You don't have to be afraid of doing something, and I found not putting too much pressure on myself really worked. I just started to try to do little bits when I felt I could.

I did a series of meditation on the 'Calm' app. This was for ten minutes a day and I would sit and listen. The app gets you to concentrate on your breathing along with imagining happy scenery. The whole aim of the exercise is to clear bad thoughts and sit and listen to the rain sounds and calming music. This really worked for me and allowed sleep during a period when I was finding it very difficult to get any rest at all.

Lavender and eucalyptus are really calming. Make sure to buy a candle or some essential oils to fill your room with lovely scents. Then, if you have not got a weighted blanket, try one. This really helped me sleep when I felt very anxious. I also bought a blindfold that you heat up in the microwave and it stays warm for 15 minutes which has helped to soothe my headaches and eye pain. I also have a Kool 'n' Soothe menthol roller for my head as well as headache strips. These provide cooling to the area for migraines and have a calming effect.

Exercise: Sit with your feelings

Make sure to find time to meditate and sit with your feelings.

- Breathe in through your nose and out through your mouth while sitting in a comfortable position.
- Have a good posture, clear your mind of any thoughts and think about the sensations running through your body.

Meditation apps do help if you want to listen to someone's voice, but if you want to do this on your own, search on YouTube for rain sounds and/or buy a white noise machine.

Exercise: My happiness list

Now you have spent time with your feelings, get your notebook and write a list of a few things that make you happy. This can be your reminder when sad times come to go back to this list and do something that makes you happy.

What does happiness look like for you? Describe your happy safe place in your notebook.

2

SHOCK AND DENIAL (THE FIRST STAGE OF GRIEF)

The eye hospital appointments got more frequent at the age of 11. By the time I was 13, my mum was letting me dye my hair every colour under the sun because she is very relaxed like that, but also because there was always this looming doubt in my life about whether I would, in fact, lose all my vision eventually. My family and I tried hard not to let it swallow our thoughts too much.

Up until around the age of 15, I managed to get through life taking my gradual sight loss on the chin because I had enough vision to get about. I could read 12-point font, bus stop and train signs, and even, in good lighting, expiry dates on food packets. There was part of me that felt invincible. Even with this really rare disease, I could still see really well. I didn't let things overly get to me day to day, but my eyesight gradually did get worse.

The year 2007 was big for me. It was the year I went to secondary school. So excited to get my brand-new uniform and small Nokia phone with a keypad, I packed my Jane Norman bag with schoolbooks that I was happy I could still read and a little bag of make-up, including some Max Factor Crème Puff powder that was definitely a shade too dark for me, and couldn't wait to go to school. I wanted more than anything to fit in, so meeting up with my long white cane instructor Terri was something that made me stand out. I hated my cane for so long because I felt like I didn't need it. I could independently walk through the corridors at school – there were a few trips and spills at times, but I did it. I think the second time I came home with a grazed elbow from a school concrete post because I misjudged how open a door was on the way to third period, was the moment my mum and dad wanted me to take cane training seriously.

'Just have it in your bag sweetheart,' my mum would always say. I felt like I wanted to dig to Australia when I used it. No one else had one and it is the most boring piece of carbon fibre that I ever laid eyes on. In my mind, only elderly people had canes, not 11-year-olds.

The only reason that I would even consider holding it back then was because Terri was teaching me how to use it away from my friends and outside of lessons.

At home, my mum had bought an eye chart that she would test me with most days and I would hate the ritual. I understood why she did it – I couldn't tell when I was losing the sight in my right eye because my left was compensating for my right, so my parents wanted to be able to help me determine changes in my vision. I found this very annoying. I would do anything to avoid talking about my sight loss outside of the hospital appointments because it felt so traumatic. Surely if I didn't acknowledge that it was happening then it wasn't going to happen. Teenage logic is just something isn't it? If I never thought about my eyes again it would be too soon.

I had so much going on in my life that, when I lost all of my sight in my right eye in the first term of school, I didn't really know how to process it. I vividly remember being at school in the girls' toilets getting my period for the first time, putting a sanitary towel in my underwear and thinking, 'Okay, so that is another new change to my body I have to deal with.' Placing the remaining packaging of my pad in the bin next to the toilet, I looked up to unlock the cubicle door and

I noticed something. The poster that I could read a week earlier was blurry. I stared and stared wishing that the image would come back, but it didn't.

The bell rang to signify that lunchtime was over and I just stood squinting for what must have only been a few minutes, but it felt like hours. My now only remaining sighted left eye started to ache. I put my bag back down on the toilet floor, stood with my back against the door and had my first-ever panic attack. I knew everyone had gone to the last lessons of the day and I was alone with my thoughts at that moment. I can't honestly put into words what it is like to lose your eyesight after going from pretty much 20:20 vision at the age of eight to now having one eye to rely on only a few years later. I felt numb. I felt scared. I went home early that day and never went in that particular cubicle again, even if it was free, because I couldn't bear not being able to see the image on the back of the cubicle door.

At this point, I was referred to Moorfields Eye Hospital in London from the eye hospital in Birmingham to get a second opinion on whether they should try to save the sight in my right eye. The surgeon who ultimately made the call that they should not operate is still my consultant now.

After months and months of monitoring both my eyes, ultimately there was nothing anyone could do. There was some talk of using a retinal buckle to hopefully regain some vision back in my right eye, but it would make that eye a lot smaller and the opinion at the time was that it would not work. After the loss of sight in my right eye, we continued to visit Moorfields regularly to watch my left eye. The consultant always talked about the dangers of an operation and how that might make me lose what little eyesight I did have. An operation, it seems, would only be a response to a severe deterioration in my eyesight as a last-ditch attempt to save it!

I always had to be really careful to avoid any impact on my head. I withdrew from PE lessons because my left retina was hanging on by a thread and I was told any impact may detach my retina and cause vision loss. I never did geography lessons because I was told the maps were hard to make accessible and required specialist skills to make them understandable by touch. To this day, I still have real problems understanding where countries are in the world!

I used to love PE, especially netball, and played in the school team at primary school with a couple of my best friends. I hated having to sit to one side and it only exacerbated the feeling of isolation. There was an incident at sports day, after I decided to sit and watch my classmates participate on the massive sports field, when I began not to be able to see the events happening all that clearly. All the students became blurry blobs on a sea of green. I couldn't even see the white spray-painted lines on the floor anymore. I realized that I was scared of any sports equipment coming anywhere near me or anyone coming near my head.

Around the time I lost sight in my right eye, I was being bullied by a girl at school. It was a really low time for me. The bullying got so bad that my parents took me out of that school and put me into a private all-girls school where I met my best friend, Vibhati. I loved being in a new environment that felt safe compared to the larger comprehensive school. Sadly, as my sight loss continued, the school building, which was an old church with echoing corridors, wooden structures and stained-glass windows, and the home to many steep staircases and winding routes, became increasingly hard to navigate. As it was a private school, this meant I wore a bright cherry-red blazer and a long mid-tone grey pleated skirt that had to be knee length. The wooden desks were like something out of Roald Dahl's *Matilda* and my maths teacher even wrote on a chalk board, which, even now, felt like I was going back in time. The new school was my security for now – I loved going to cooking class with my Little Red Riding Hood basket and going into science with my long white lab coat on.

During this time of my life, I really excelled at school. I would go home for hours at night and make sure my homework was done. I made my workbooks really neat…I have always been conscientious like that. Unfortunately, I came to realize that getting the rehabilitation and special educational needs (SEN) specialists in to help my learning was a lot harder in this setting because it wasn't government-funded.

I found myself at my third and final secondary school at the end of Year 9, aged 14. I had to switch schools around this time as there was no visual impairment unit at the all-girls school and my vision was just getting so bad. Not that I wanted anything to do with a visual impairment unit whatsoever… The thought of having to be associated with those words filled me with utter dread. My mum fought for months to get me into this secondary school because there were no state school places available and we lived just outside the catchment area. Mum even had to attend court hearings to make a case for why my sister Alice and I deserved a place at the school together.

My first day was interesting. I stood outside in the playground and was surrounded by other students just peering at me. This was the second time in a few years that I had been the new girl so at this point it felt quite normal to change schools and introduce myself to classmates, which is how I met my best friend Connie. It was quite nice to distract myself with a new environment to learn when I had so many different memories of losing my vision in the other schools. I could almost reinvent myself and pretend I wasn't losing my sight because I hid the fact that I couldn't see to everyone. None of my new classmates knew at all. I almost had two personas: the Lucy who could be outgoing, happy and carefree; and the Lucy who thought about nothing other than enlargements of textbooks, stressed about knowing where I was in the corridors, and held her long white cane and felt sick – the anxious version of me who had to learn how to live in a sighted world with a visual impairment with no manual or guidebook.

I now had a card that my special educational needs coordinator (SENCO) gave me that got me out of lessons five minutes early so I could avoid the crush in the corridors. I was starting to bump into things a lot more now. It was a daily task to get teachers to remember to enlarge my documents. The time when my French teacher told me that she hadn't had time before the lesson to make it bigger so I would 'just have to make do' really sticks in my mind. I was only 14 years old and I suddenly had to understand how to advocate for myself overnight. I didn't know what to say to this teacher. I thought that I was an inconvenience, making her job even harder. I didn't want to speak up because she was busy teaching. I found that it was taking me longer to complete classwork than the other students because I didn't just have the learning to think about, so I took it home and made sure I had digested everything that the teacher had said.

My additional access needs allowed me to access everything like the other students, but I started to feel guilty that I was asking for different materials just because I wanted to be equal. It seemed as if I was always asking for enlarged copies of things or for diagrams to be explained. I always knew the teachers were busy and meant well, but my access needs were often the last thing they did after the rest of the class was sorted. Worse still, at times the teachers would forget to bring enlarged print or send me the materials before the lesson. Sometimes I strained my eyes to look at the pages so much because I didn't want to make a fuss. At times I would come home with such painful eyes. My mum once turned to me and told me that they both looked bloodshot.

Sometimes I just wanted to scream and I felt so frustrated sitting in class and being unable to join in the lesson. I often had teaching assistants with me as well, who were lovely, but had varying degrees of computer technology skills. I used to feel so sad that the Lucy who had grown up learning computer skills from a very young age just couldn't get straight in and sort stuff out. Instead, I always had to wait and had a steep learning curve working out how to communicate clearly and get my point across to an adult who was helping me. This was a weird thing to get used to because adults used to tell me what to do, not the other way around. Suddenly adults were asking me what I needed and I felt a weight of responsibility. Don't get me wrong, I totally love the teaching assistants I had – I was just mourning the loss of being able to look at a screen. Many of my assistants went above and beyond what they needed to do and will remain firm friends.

As my eyesight declined even more, I spent a long time memorizing how many steps it was between each classroom door, so I didn't have to use my cane. Everyday tasks were becoming harder to complete as I was clinging on to sighted ways of completing them. I just wanted everything to go back to the way it was. I didn't want to have to explain what I needed to yet another teacher just to get by. It all became so tiring that some nights after school I would fall asleep as soon as I got home.

At 16 years old I developed a cataract in my left eye. This made the lens of my eye gradually very cloudy over time. I managed to hold out not having any operations on my eye so I could get through my GCSEs, even though I struggled so much. Every week things around me would get more and more blurry. I remember being in one of my first English literature A-level lessons with my laptop out having enlarged the novel *Birdsong* so big that the whole room could probably see it. I had to invert my computer screen so I had a black page with white bold writing on it otherwise I could not read it. I remember highlighting a sentence in order to write a note about it and the yellow highlighting tool hurt my eyes. I used a black marker pen in all of my schoolbooks and just felt thankful that I could still see my own writing. It got to the point at the beginning of my A levels when I started not to be able to see the pen anymore. I had left the cataract so long that I was just walking around in a hazy fog.

The cataract surgeon said that they wanted to hold off for as long as they could because there was a real risk that removing the cataract would also detach my retina that was hanging on for dear life. Eventually, the time came for me to have the cataract operation. I woke up afterwards, so happy to see my sister's spots and my mum's wrinkles. I still remember it as one of the happiest moments of my life. The surgeon said the operation went well and all of us cried with happiness that day.

Four months later, my mum and I hopped on the train from Birmingham to London as we always did after an op to check on how my vision was doing. On that occasion, I remember not being able to read as far down my eye chart as I usually did before I had my cataract. I remember saying to my mum that it was weird. We asked for more regular check-ups as we were worried, and we were right to be.

When we were travelling home that day, Mum and I knew I was going to have a tough few months ahead of me, so she wanted to take me on a shopping trip to cheer me up. We went to the Bullring shopping centre in Birmingham and my mum took me into a

Dr Martens shop and purchased me my first-ever pair. I had been looking at these black boots in the window for months and months. We also went to Miss Selfridge and she bought me this beautiful blue and white peplum jumper that I cannot ever get rid of – it still lives in mine and Ollie's wardrobe to this day.

Speaking of lovely Ollie, we met at the age of 16 after joining a local amateur dramatics club local to my home in Birmingham. It was hosted in a little old building named Highbury Little Theatre. I would go every Sunday with my sister and friends. Ollie lived on the other side of the city to this theatre, but heard about the club because the person running it – Jane – was a close family friend. She had made a call for more male performers as we were doing a production named 'Our House' by Madness. Ollie decided to respond to Jane's call for cast members and played a Scottish man named Callum in the play. We will never forget his amazing tweed plaid trousers and his very questionable Scottish accent. One evening, Ollie met me in Sutton Park and we went to see *Ted* in the cinema, and we started dating.

I want to say that my sight loss didn't play a part in our journey, but it really did. When I went in for my cataract operation I decided to break it off with Ollie quite early on in the relationship and told him that he couldn't deal with my sight loss so young. He kept chatting to me and I remember talking to him on Facebook Messenger late into the night before my cataract operation. He never stopped supporting me. We ultimately got back together because Ollie didn't see my sight loss as a barrier; he just wanted to support me. In February 2013 we were sitting in my then bedroom at my family home. It was really dark. Ollie was about to walk to the train station as he always did to get back home and I turned to look at him and said, 'Ollie, you are glowing.' My bedside lamp was behind him.

He turned to me and said, 'What do you mean, Lu?'

I didn't really know how to answer other than it looked like there were two of him. It freaked me out enough to go straight down to my dad and tell him.

The next thing I knew, I was being told that my remaining retina in my left eye was detaching. We'd been warned this might happen after my cataract operation, but we had decided to do the surgery anyway. The following weeks are all a blur. One of the last TV programmes I saw was *Comic Relief*. I sat super close to the TV – right in front of the screen – and took in every detail I possibly could. I stared so hard because, deep down, I knew it would be the last time I ever saw the TV. All I wished for in that moment was more time. I thought about all of the lovely things I was lucky enough to have laid my eyes on, but I couldn't help but make a list of the things that I would never see again.

The list included the Northern Lights, the solar system, Mount Vesuvius, the landscapes of the sheep in a field in Wales, my 30-year-old face and my pores, my wedding day, my children's faces, my new houses, rainbows…When I listen to it now, it reminds me of the pain I felt writing it and I would never have imagined how differently I would feel about both not being able to see these things but also how my memory has faded. If I could have told myself at that point that I would be able to adapt to a different way of thinking it would have helped me so much. For example, now I think about how the colours in a rainbow make me feel happy and positive rather than the actual colours themselves.

That was how I found myself in the inpatient ward at Moorfields Eye Hospital speaking to my amazing consultant about hope and listening to Jason Walker as I waited for the operation I thought would break me.

Finally, at around 6pm, the slowest day of my life was over and my name was called.

The next thing I remember is waking up after being given really strong drugs and lying on the spot with a fan on my legs. I was coming round, but I couldn't see anything at all. The first thing I thought was: 'Fuck, I am trapped.' But then I felt my face and I had a bandage on my eye. I heard loads of voices around me, but it was like a nightmare. Before I went down for the operation, Mum and Kaz had told me they would find me as soon as I came out of theatre and they promised they wouldn't leave the hospital because I was so scared. They never left and were asking all the staff who would talk to them where I was. They constantly checked around corridors and waited by lifts until I heard them both calling my name and my chest heaved with relief.

I kept telling myself that when the bandage was removed I would be able to see again. I didn't know if that was true, but it had to be, otherwise I would not get through the next few minutes, let alone hours, waiting for someone to update me on how the surgery had gone.

Very late on Friday night, we were told that the operation had gone well and the consultant would see me in the morning. I was also told that a silicone oil bubble was in my eye – the surgeon had had to cut away more retina than he had wanted to – and that I had to lie on my front for several months in order to give my eyesight the best chance. After that, I remember feeling oddly happy, but in a hysterical way. I phoned my dad and sister and my best friend Connie and, of course, Ollie to tell them it all went well and I couldn't wait to get my patch off in the morning.

There was no way I was staying in the hospital overnight. After more than 14 hours in the hospital, I wanted to borrow the pillow that I was face-planting and check-in to the hotel across the road. But the hospital had no head rests available to loan for the night. My mum and Kaz went on a quest to find a pillow to loan, but the only one available was the one I was already lying on. After a lot of back and forth, Mum and Kaz managed to convince the nurse that we were only taking it over the road and we would promise to keep it safe and bring it back to them in the morning. Mum even showed them proof of our appointment on Saturday morning. I felt so out of it that arguing over a pillow was making me a little hysterical after all of the emotion the day had held.

I will never understand why the nurse didn't have
more compassion after we'd had such a traumatic day.

I honestly felt like a shell of my former self.
I stumbled out of that hospital with a patch on my
eye, only just about managing to put one foot in
front of the other because I was grasping on to Mum
and Kaz's arms. I was terrified as we emerged out
of the eye hospital and onto the pavement of the
busy city road. My ears were so overwhelmed.
Everything felt so loud. All I wanted to do was
shuffle my way back home. I felt myself walking
so slowly because I was so scared. Every car that
went by felt like it was going to hit me. I had no
concept of how far away anything was from me
because I had never just relied completely on my
other senses to navigate before. Every dip or pothole
in the road felt like a mountain. Every loud person
on the phone or talking in the street was talking
to me. Police car sirens echoed through my skull.
An overgrown bush brushed my arm, but it could
have been anything. Panic and shock set in at the
littlest of noises. Bees were now jackhammers. I was
a rabbit caught in the headlights, always on guard,
heart racing at the slightest of noises. Total sensory
overload set in and nothing could have prepared me

for that moment. This was the start of me feeling sick for many months.

We finally got into the hotel, and relief set in because the operation had gone well. There was also a lot of hope that I would have my patch removed and be able to see okay. I called Ollie again feeling optimistic and managed to chat about his day because I wanted to distract myself with lovely things.

We slept okay that night, all things considered, as we were all so sleep-deprived from the night before. Sometimes, when the odds are stacked against you, all you have is rebellious hope. This is what allowed us to rest that night. The term, coined by the late Dame Deborah James, allowed me to believe that hope isn't a bad thing even when times are tough.

When we all went back to the hospital in the morning it was truly the worst day I have ever lived, and most likely will be up there with the worst day I will ever live in my whole life. We arrived at the hospital early – it is always the Edwards way to be early – but, despite this, the staff said we had missed the doctor who had gone upstairs to do his ward round and we should wait for him to come back down. We waited and waited for what seemed like hours. The nurse came and removed my top bandage. I was so distressed as all I could see were blurry blobs. I thought I would see way more than I did, but it was like I was viewing the world through a slit. As I sat processing this change in vision, Kaz said to me and Mum that sitting downstairs we might be forgotten – she felt that we were 'out of sight and out of mind'. We were beyond exhausted and I wanted nothing more than to get some more explanations about what had happened in surgery and to be discharged, so we all decided to go upstairs to where the clinic was running and I sat right in front of the consultant's door.

I was desperately hoping that I would find my surgeon who I had known since I was 11 years old, but, given that it was a Saturday morning, we were not sure if he would visit. I was hoping that he might be able to tell me this wasn't real, that something might change. Eventually, he came in wearing his jeans as it was the weekend and my mum said, 'I have never been so pleased to see someone as much in my life.' He cared. We all knew this was going to be a hard meeting and he delivered the worst news ever to me and my family.

My mum and Kaz guided me through a busy clinic full of patients into a very empty consulting room with nothing but desks and eye equipment. My surgeon turned to Mum and Kaz and said, 'She will be lucky to have anything by December.'

I just stared blankly out of my new reality and felt empty. For the first time, I saw darkness like never before. I thought back to all of the moments I had moaned about my visual impairment and felt sick. I felt betrayed that everyone had been saying for so many hours that the operation had gone well, but then, when they took the patch off, I could see close to nothing.

I guess no one would really be able to predict exactly what vision I would have when taking off my gauze, so I lived on a different plane of existence for quite a few hours. Maybe it was just that I couldn't truly believe what the consultants had said to me when they warned me in the pre-op consultation that they would have to cut away quite a lot of my eye to save it. I don't think I could really take that in because, in my mind, it was all going to be okay – in a weird way, I didn't let myself go there. I couldn't comprehend what true blindness was going to be like; I couldn't really understand what could happen so I couldn't really think about it.

I felt intense sorrow wash over me like a tidal wave. I felt sad that my consultant was now asking me if I could see how many fingers he was holding up. I had such little vision that I couldn't see faces anymore.

I couldn't see roads or pictures or my phone. I couldn't see the pattern on the scarf that Kaz had given me less than 24 hours ago. I couldn't see the detail on my own hand, the laces on the trainers I was wearing or the blue sky out of the window. In that moment, I realized that I was never going to see another fluffy cloud, a beautiful flower or a sunny day, or a rainy one for that matter. I couldn't speak or cry. I just sat there. I don't even remember how many fingers my surgeon was holding up. I managed to tell him correctly, but that didn't make me feel any better. I kept holding my hand out wishing I could see my fingernails, but I couldn't. I thought that, if I did it for long enough, the picture would come back to me. I just wanted a time machine. I could see the light coming from the window, but not the window itself. I could see the colour of someone's T-shirt who was standing incredibly close to me, but nothing else. The world was now blurry blobs. I could see motion, but couldn't tell what was moving. In a world where we can be anything, I had to be blind. I wanted to run away from my own body, but I was trapped inside. I was now living in the same body I had been for 17 years, but it had changed overnight. I didn't recognize myself anymore. I didn't speak properly for days. I was just in shock.

My mum remembers just being so relieved that my surgeon had come in, but we were all in shock. I think Mum and Kaz went into coping mode. Mum was in disbelief that this was actually happening and I just didn't know what to say to her. Honestly, after chatting to Mum and Kaz since then, we don't remember much else.

When it came to the practicalities of getting me home, we paid for first-class train tickets as they were cheaper on a Saturday and Kaz bought me a neck pillow that I lay on during the train ride and beyond. In order for the silicone bubble to have the best chance of pushing my retina back to where it was meant to be, I was told to lie on my front for two months. I was also told that I would never have the bubble taken out. I can confirm that it has never been taken out because it is still in my left eye as I write this book. I don't have any memory of this train ride, but I was chatting to Kaz the other day and she says that she gets sad when she remembers how wet the train table was that day from my tears. She said I cried all the way home. In the days that followed I didn't know what to do with myself. There was nowhere to turn: no resources online; no support or aftercare from the hospital; no one in my life who could understand what sight loss meant. It was just me and my family against the world.

Mum slept with me in my bed for weeks because I didn't want to be alone. Kaz came over every day and bought me different smelly shampoos and products to help me know what I was holding. Dad went into sort mode and bought me an over-the-bed table for me to rest my head on during the day. Ollie came round to see me a few days later. I distinctly remember not being able to wash my hair for a few weeks, but I wanted to look nice for him, so Mum put my greasy hair in a French plait. I wore a baseball T-shirt from Hollister with blue arms and a white top and black leggings. I felt embarrassed that I couldn't look like a normal teenager in that moment. I felt guilty that I was bringing Ollie into my very complicated and sad situation. Some part of me wanted to tell him to run and save himself. I think I did say that very thing occasionally for a few months, but he kept coming to see me. Ollie was only 16 years old and he looked at me and said, 'I am never leaving you Lucy, I love you.'

I felt like the luckiest girl in the world, but I knew that I wouldn't find myself again for many, many months to come. I don't think you can ever be the same person again after such a loss. Something died that day for me. Every morning afterwards I woke up being reminded of my sight loss – with every drink I made and every person in my life I could no longer see, and knowing that every memory I went on to make would now make my heart ache with pain.

THE IMMEDIACY OF TRAUMA

How do you deal with loss and trauma in the immediacy of the moment? This is going to be different for every one of us. For me, I crumbled slowly. For many months, I didn't want to admit that I was blind. I refused to learn any screen reader. I refused to go out on my own. I refused to make my own drinks or food because all of these tasks meant that I needed to face the fact that I couldn't see anymore. If I didn't do anything then I didn't have to face what had happened, that anything was happening. I just waited for every minute to pass and hoped I would get through the hours.

My life as I knew it was over and the grief was all-consuming. There were hours when I just sat in bed staring. There were moments when I tried to look at everything in my room that I could remember seeing. I would force myself to keep the visuals alive in my mind by obsessing over tiny details that I could remember from a week earlier.

As soon as it happened, I tried to block out all my emotion for months. I had hours when I couldn't stop hysterically crying and obsessing over every detail, but I just did everything in my power to fill my day with people to talk to. If I wasn't on the phone, I would be with my family. I found that I didn't really want to see anyone other than people who were incredibly close to me during this time. If they didn't live this horror with me then I couldn't see them again. I felt so disconnected with who I was so it made me feel better if I knew people understood – my family and school friends and that's it. I know this sounds weird to write down, but everyone in my life who had not been through this day with me was toast.

When something like this winds you, it feels so drastic and you see life in black and white; nothing was grey for me anymore. I became less tolerant and didn't recognize the Lucy who was hurtling towards me. That is why I blocked her out for so long. I wasn't ready to be blind so it took my mind a year or so to catch up with reality.

It took me some time to realize that I was managing

a traumatic event, which, on reflection, seems very strange when you put the fact that I lost the rest of my vision overnight following surgery down on paper in front of me. I was told that if I didn't have my operation I would lose the rest of my eyesight, but the reality of that hadn't sunk in really, so when I came out of surgery and took that bandage off I was shocked beyond belief. My initial recovery from surgery was dealt with in the usual loving way from all those around me. After the initial rest and recuperation that inevitably followed an operation such as this, I started to try to work out what life held for me next. Knowing very little about dealing with trauma in the short term, I reacted by trying to solve things. This would range from trying to use my computer again, working out the details of VoiceOver on my computer and phone, learning new voiceover systems such as JAWS and developing complicated methods of cooking, cleaning and managing everyday life. It very quickly became exhausting, and every time I couldn't manage a task it took me back continuously to the trauma of my sight loss.

I have thought about grief lots and it's only as the continued trauma of losing my eyesight remained as the focal point of my life that I began to think that it would be impossible to move on through the grief process and from the past into the present. I had taken steps to rest and initially listened to all of the advice so kindly framed by those around me. 'Take things slowly', 'Manage small things at a time', 'Don't be too hard on yourself because you can't do something', 'Rest, take it easy' are some of the things my loved ones would say. I tried so hard to do this, taking steps to enjoy things I could do more easily as a non-sighted person. I booked days at the spa, took some gentle walks and, on reflection, it all helped. The feeling of shock and isolation was so new that I didn't really know what to do. The times when I rested and decided to be gentle to myself were definitely preferable to the manic Lucy who was trying to solve everything! The panic that would follow when I was unable to complete things was a new and strange sensation having grown up as a relatively confident child.

It's always a good idea to get help if you need to – I have definitely required professional help over the years. Here are some of the things I do in addition to try to reduce my anxiety on a day-to-day basis.

Exercise: Coping with panic attacks

I use these simple thoughts and techniques when I am finding things particularly difficult:

- Always try to remind yourself that the attack is not likely to last a long time.
- Breathe in and out slowly. I sometimes count between the 'in' and 'out' breath.
- Sit quietly, if possible, and focus on what's going on around you as the anxiety starts to calm.
- Try to have regular counselling appointments and make sure you talk to a professional.

Exercise: Managing anxiety

Can you reduce exposure to the three anxiety-provoking things? List how you can do this for each.

List two to three things in your notebook that you know will likely cause anxiety and write about them.

Write down how you can manage the anxiety if/ when you are exposed. For example, I recorded my feelings in a journal when I started my new job at the BBC. This helped me to figure out some of my thought patterns and anxiety about work.

Exercise: Dealing with trauma

I try to think about the difference between trauma and grief, as it can be very hard to distinguish between them for me. It took a long time for me to realize that I needed trauma counselling after it became more evident that I was unable to move forward from the event of sight loss and felt it defining me. I guess that really is the point I want to make.

Take some time to write down your feelings associated with the loss you have experienced. They might include irritability, difficulty sleeping, lack of concentration, self-destructive patterns of behaviour, being ready for danger and feelings of guilt or shame.

Draw a picture of or imagine yourself walking down a path and the things you dream about for the future are at the end. On the way to the dream at the end of the road, you face obstacles but are not able to walk around and reach the end. Write down what obstacles are in your way. Can you even see the end of the path? If not, this might mean that your trauma is all-consuming at the moment.

This kind of exercise might help you to see if you are able to make the journey or are stuck in the mud at the moment. If you are writing more about one type of thing, analyse why that might be and take it to counselling. This was a great thought-starter for me when trying to understand my trauma triggers.

3

THE EARLY DAYS:
PAIN AND GUILT
(THE SECOND STAGE
OF GRIEF)

'You look beautiful,' my sister Alice remarked as she smiled at me. It is noon on 13 April 2013. It was like any other day – just another girly shopping trip we had embarked on together. We both stood in front of a tall mirror in a narrow, dimly lit changing room, but today, for the first time, her words didn't seem to sink in. She grasped my hand tightly waiting to hear what I thought about the outfit she had picked off the rails for me. I zoned out a little. All I could hear was the booming speakers, other girls laughing as they strutted up the aisle past our cubicle in high heels and hangers falling.

Tears brimmed in my poorly eyes and only one question flooded my mind: 'What do I look like now?' A simple trip had turned into a question that swallowed me whole. A little over two weeks earlier I pretty much lost my eyesight overnight. Alice had taken me shopping to take my mind off the trauma. I don't think any of us knew what to do in the weeks following my operation. There was now an empty void we were all scrambling around to fill. The laughter of the other teens in the shop pierced through me. I used to be like them when I came shopping. I felt so lost in a situation I usually felt the most at home in. Alice touched my arm and asked, 'Luce, are you okay? What do you think of the outfit?'

What do I think? I thought. Alice stared back at my reflection and we both stood there frozen. I tried to concentrate, but I was on planet Mars. It felt lonely inside my head – redefining what I thought about myself was going to be a long journey. My heart started to race. Since my sight loss, I had been attempting to do everyday activities and they had ended up being too emotionally exhausting. This was just another activity I had to add to the list. I couldn't run away fast enough. It was a new way of life that

I couldn't accept. I started shaking. My body couldn't comprehend where to put all of this emotion.

After all, I had spent 17 years of my life enjoying the visual world. At that moment, everything felt so definite. My sister pulled me out of my daze by giving me one of her warm, tight hugs. She held on to me a little longer and whispered, 'It's going to be okay. Let's go home.' A bit of retail therapy together always used to work, but even my beautiful sister couldn't plaster over my scars this time. To Alice, I was just Lucy. Her sister. She wanted to remind me that we could still do things. My eyes never changed the way she saw me. I would always be beautiful in her eyes, even though a part of me had broken. She did everything in her power to remind me that Lucy still existed.

I felt silly for not being able to partake in what should and would have been such a simple task two weeks earlier: looking in a mirror. Memory after memory bubbled up in my mind. What did I wish I saw as my last glance? My heart ached. I was out of tears and the whole world had turned off everysingle light. No one wanted to give me a candle. My heart broke into a thousand pieces, and I was too full of sorrow to have the energy to pick up the shards. Time slows down when you are in pain.

Alice guided me out of the changing room. I took her right elbow with my left hand and we walked beside each other. Shuffling through the shopping centre to the car felt so odd. Families chatted and joked, eating food in the plaza as we passed. Life felt so vibrant for them, so happy and colourful. 'L.I.F.E.G.O.E.S.O.N.' by songwriter Charlie Fink and performed by Noah and the Whale was a track I played on repeat. I used to sing the lyrics: 'What you don't have now will come back again.' I felt so betrayed that I used to think like this. My 16-year-old fun-loving self was so foreign to me. How could I ever be okay without my vision? Visual memory was fading fast, but the visual world continued without me. I craved visual stimulation. The life I used to know was over. There was nothing I could do or say for it to be different.

In the coming months, various family members kept repeating 'there is more to life than sight'. For a while, I didn't believe them. I don't think I really wanted to take advice from those who didn't feel as trapped as me in that moment. I felt that no one around me understood because they had their vision. The loss, shock and grief of losing my main sense so quickly and traumatically were hindering any ability of mine to think positively about sight loss. I denied it had happened for a while. I bargained with myself that surely I could live vicariously through my sighted sister, but it wasn't making me happy. My natural response was to try to look at something, but when I couldn't, I felt inept.

The longer I didn't accept myself, the longer I beat myself up – it was no way to live a happy life.

I had to live out all my firsts again. Pouring a drink, making beans on toast or texting a friend was painful. I spent months at a time in bed as I cried into a tub of Ben & Jerry's ice cream. Every day merged into one. I was scared to do anything or go anywhere because I didn't want to make memories I couldn't see. All I thought about was everything I didn't have anymore.

My teaching assistant, Maxine, and I became so close and she really helped me get through this time of my life. I had to retake one year of sixth form as my eye operation meant that I didn't do any of my A-level exams in May 2013 because I was too ill. I found myself sitting in classes with my sister's friends while watching my school year go to university. I dictated all my exams to Maxine because I wasn't that proficient in Braille or my tech in order to do my exams independently. I felt guilty that I hadn't learned Braille or technology more as I had been encouraged to do now it was all the more painful trying to complete new tasks without sight. Maxine sat with me in my exams and I had 100 per cent extra time meaning that some English literature and history papers were spread over two days. The visual impairment unit that I once didn't want to be associated with was my lifeline.

I only took three subjects for A level so that meant lots of free periods. Sometimes I would learn Braille or touch-typing. Sometimes I would have mobility lessons with lovely Terri. Sometimes I would complete some homework with Maxine and she would offer me a few toffee sweets and a cuppa. I actually never drank tea before the lovely ladies started giving it to me. When Maxine wasn't in, I used to have Ange. Ange was fun and we often had a laugh together during school, which was a relief from all the serious times. Without these women advocating for me and getting me all the resources I needed to get through, it would have been even harder to watch my friends leave school a year earlier than me.

I remember looking around the University of Oxford with Ange. We went on the train and attended the open day. After a quick pit stop for scones, we walked to one of the colleges. I mentioned to one of the professors that I would be bringing my guide dog

Olga. They said they had never had a guide dog before. Walking around the croquet lawn I realized that it may not be a place for me when I started asking where Olga would do a poo, and the sound of horror in the student guide's voice that I would ever insinuate that a dog would poo on the croquet lawn was so hilarious. I managed to hold in my laughter until I left the building.

Ange and I did have a giggle that day. This was the first time I really thought about university differently. The main route out of school was getting into a good university and then going on to get a good job. I still thought that this was important, but, after losing my main sense, I really valued happiness over struggling to force my way into environments that didn't necessarily suit me. Oxford could have suited me if I was willing to educate every single person I saw about my blindness, but why spend all my energy doing this when I needed every single bit of time spent on doing my law degree? Inevitably there were going to be lots of inaccessible intranet systems and diagrams so I thought it would be best to go to a university with some more disabled students in attendance, which is sad in itself to have to write. I wish the world was less judgemental. There are so many people who judge a book by its cover and I am now so thankful that I see the pages first and never see the cover. It is a part of life that I value the most.

Life continued and Ollie took me out on our first date after my operation in August 2013. We went to an audio-described showing of the film *About Time*. He knew I love Richard Curtis films so wanted to treat me. We got in the cinema, grabbed an audio-described headset and went into the film. Halfway through, my headset ran out of power. It cut out during the scene when the main character goes back to visit his dad before he dies. At this point I felt guilty every day that everyone around me had to help me out all the time so I just didn't say anything to Ollie. I felt so ashamed to ask for anything. I came out and eventually told Ollie that the tech had failed me.

In those early days I never wanted to admit my struggles because I wasn't used to having to struggle in this way. Everything I went to do felt so weird. Nothing was normal. I couldn't even go on a teenage date properly. I could not run away from access issues or discrimination. At this time in my life every access issue was a big deal. I took everything to heart and it crippled my confidence.

Ollie described every inch of a new environment to me until one day I realized that I couldn't possibly take in all of the visual information I used to because it was weighing down my mind, making me so tired, taking up all of mine and Ollie's conversation space, and making Ollie think of every detail when he could just be having a good time describing the main things around us more casually. I guess in life you get into a rhythm with everything eventually. Ollie and I didn't go to the cinema again for a date until around five years later when we went to see the new *Incredibles* movie with Ollie's sister when we lived in London. In some ways, I cannot believe that it took me so long to go to a cinema again, but, in other ways, shutting it out helped me work out what I thought of audio description in my own time.

I felt like every day I was just surviving, not thriving. All I could do to cope was simply go to school and get home again. For years, I had nightmares every night of the patch coming off my eye in the hospital. I would scream with terror in my dream and wake up sweating. For many years, I would open my eyes only to remember that I couldn't see. It was like Groundhog Day. I couldn't stop this intrusive dream or thoughts until I started to open up and talk about my feelings a little with a counsellor. I felt sick for years.

Most of the time I would walk around like a zombie and have moments when I forced myself to cope. Like when my friends invited me to the pub for a drink. Alice used to make me look so glam – she still does! She picked my outfit, and my mum did my hair. They became my mirrors; my everything. I wouldn't feel okay unless Alice said I looked good. I was so lucky to have a solid group of friends that did a collection for me when I became blind and were with me when I got my long white cane out for the first time in the school corridor. My bestie Connie went into all my lessons and recorded them with my Dictaphone. Both her and my other bestie Beth never stopped texting, even though I couldn't bring myself to reply because I felt so low. It meant the world to me that they never stopped trying. They knew I was in there. They just knew they had to wait it out.

All my friends went off to university and I went a few times to their halls. I was happy when I saw them, but couldn't shake the feeling of sadness when I got home. There was one moment when I arranged with Beth to go to her second-year house in Leeds. I cancelled at the last minute because I felt too sick to go on the train. It was self-sabotage because I truly didn't believe I deserved to have a good time with my friends. Back then, all I could think about was all of the misery I would bring to the party if I went to see them. I wanted them to live their lives. I felt guilty that they had to guide me when they were all in a new city, with new friends, living their new lives. There was no way that I wanted to bring my dark cloud over their new experiences. I loved them so much that I wanted to protect them from my true sadness. I thought that if I didn't reply they would be able to be happy and get on with their lives. I didn't feel envious of them because I could see that they were just living their lives. Every cell in my being wished that I was with them when they invited me out, but I just knew that, if I went, I would probably get a little too drunk and be a handful.

I recall one New Year's Eve when all my friends came home for Christmas. I was so excited to be partying with them, but I puked in the toilet before midnight and they had to move the party to Beth's house. I do not recommend drinking while on strong antidepressants. I was glad that happened in my home town rather than in another city.

I know my beautiful friends would have preferred me to be with them, but I just couldn't be. Some nights I would want to text them but couldn't bring myself to. And that continued until I was about 19. I used to have so many messages on my notes pages ready to send, but I reread them so many times before I never inevitably clicked send.

I gradually started to learn how to do things, like wash my clothes, independently again. I could make a few meals, but liked to eat the same dinner quite a lot because consistency made me less angry at myself and brought on less comparison in my mind of how I used to do things. For a solid year and a half, I made myself baked beans, potatoes and cheese in my talking microwave. Mum placed a massive order on the Royal National Institute of Blind People (RNIB) website with lots of gadgets to make me feel more independent and the microwave was one. Mum also tried to get me to eat something different, but I just couldn't – and I always had to finish it off with a Mars Bar ice cream. I wanted to obsessively control the things I could because something had been taken from me.

I eventually started law school, but was so ill I dropped out of not one but two universities. Not because I couldn't do the work, but because I just needed time to grieve what had happened to me. When I was finishing school, I was quickly into exam season. I had no real time to chat about my feelings towards being blind; only how to cope with being blind and taking classes and exams at school to get by. I found myself comparing my past life so much. Mum and Dad were starting to get really worried about me always being in my PJs and drinking four cans of Diet Coke a day. There were many nights when they brought up gently with me about different higher education paths I might want to go down, but I got very stressed every time we talked about me dropping out of university because I felt like a failure. I developed irritable bowel syndrome (IBS). I was constantly asleep day and night. My family were desperately trying to build in routines and happy things within my day.

Ollie came to live in the flat attached to my family home when he was back from university in the summer. There were rarely any moments of happiness back then, but, when Ollie arrived, I felt like a part of me came alive again. We spent every waking moment together and because we were only seventeen, having a place we could call our own was really special. Ollie saw all sides of me too back then, which was so important because a lot of the time I was sad. We started our YouTube channel 'Yesterday's Wishes' because I wanted to put my mind to something. Turning the camera on led to some of my only happy moments. Ollie edited all my videos back then and the whole premise of the channel was to not wish for yesterday but instead just look for a better tomorrow. It was a glimmer of hope that life was going to be all right.

I used to feel so guilty for having happy moments because I thought that leaving the old me behind was betraying everything I had ever known. Sadness would hit me at the weirdest of times. We would walk up the road and, because I couldn't see the road signs, I would cry and have to turn back. I would be brushing my teeth and feel physical pain when I squeezed the toothpaste onto my brush because I wanted to see it.

This is when true grief set in. I couldn't be happy without thinking that, even though I had a moment of happiness, life was still ultimately sad and, in my view, never really going to be okay without eyesight. Some days I wanted to cry all day. Other days I would ask Ollie why he wanted to be with a blind person like me. I truly did not understand why anyone would love me. I recall 2014–2016 being my worst years. At this point, I went into the 'having-to-accept-that-this-has-happened-to-me' phase. I would obsessively google 'cures for blindness', to which there were none for my type of blindness.

I gained quite a lot of weight in a short period of time because I wasn't exercising. In many ways, I didn't value my life or my body. I couldn't be left alone for long periods because that meant I would have to think about my feelings. I was suicidal for months. In the first few weeks after I lost my vision, I could block it out much more because I had recent visual memories to draw on. I had recent things in my mind that had happened, and I felt like not a lot had moved on without me. But, as time went by and my friends got a new haircut or Alice dyed her hair a different colour or someone looked at a picture of Ollie and commented on how he looked so different to his 16-year-old self, I would hold it together in the moment but not be okay for days and days after – even weeks sometimes.

It was painful to sit at a table hearing about all my friends' new friends as they would share pictures. They would never leave me out and always describe, but I felt empty. I overanalysed my reactions to them because I wanted to be happy for them. There were happy moments back then, like being at a party or celebrating something, but after the day had passed, I always knew there were going to be several weeks where I overthought everything. Like my first-ever Christmas when I was registered blind, for example.

Mum and Dad had bought a really smelly Christmas tree and really bright lights – I could see light back then as I still had some light perception – so that I could experience some festive, sighted magic. I remember opening my presents as usual with the four of us and, of course, Nan and Kaz in the morning, but asking myself why we still used wrapping paper. I didn't verbalize this because it was a sad moment for me, but what I really loved was gifting Ollie and my family things.

I wanted to change up Christmas a bit the year after, so Ollie and I focused on cooking. Also, because I was still getting used to my environment, I went through a phase of smashing lots of baubles and got quite upset, so Ollie bought me tactile decorations like the cute little Paperchase sprouts with googly eyes that I could feel. It was really sad for many years trying to define what all these new celebrations were. Even now I have to admit that even though I don't feel anywhere near as grief-stricken as I was back then, what will always make me sad until the day I am no longer here is that I will never be able to see Christmas again. Or my birthday. Big celebrations will always kick me in the gut. At the time of writing this, Ollie and I are also planning our wedding. This will be the best day of my life. I know that for certain. I will be marrying my best friend and soulmate, but I will have to live with the fact that I will never see his face on that day. When we start a family, I will never see how much our children look like my lovely Ollie.

Grief is forever. It comes in waves. I am thankful that I don't seem to have days and days of sadness and grief anymore, but what I would say is that I have now learned how to deal with it in the best way I can. In life we all live multiple truths. I can love being blind and hate being blind. I can appreciate all the great things it has enabled me to harness in life, but I can also always grieve and have moments of longing for the things I will never get back. I would say that this stage of grief is the one I personally frequent the most, but it may be different for you. It is perfectly okay to sit in your grief for a while, but in the next chapter we will chat more about how you must not let grief take hold forever. This is hard to do, but let's chat.

HOW TO ASK FOR HELP AND NOT PUSH PEOPLE AWAY

Being a very independent person asking for help was perhaps one of the most difficult aspects of sight loss for me. In the early days, it seemed as if I was forever asking for something. I decided at times that I would rather go without or stop doing things than ask for more help. I would often contemplate being in a situation and think about how I wouldn't enjoy it because I would have to ask for something. Worse still was the idea of stopping someone else enjoying themselves because of me. Asking for help was something I just didn't want to do. As a result, I found myself pushing people away and becoming more and more isolated. This was such a strong feeling that I would rather have the fear of missing out on events than be subjected to the desperate emotions generated by my perceived lack of independence. Maybe part of this was still about hating who I was and feeling a sense of deep shame. It didn't matter that others around me were saying they were happy to help, I wasn't happy to receive the well-meaning assistance.

Gradually, though, as I started to accept my new life, I began to realize that every person is dependent on others in some practical ways. I then started to work out for myself what things I would structure sighted assistance for and organize other activities so that I could complete them independently. I still have a feeling of elation when I do things without help, but I am also able to take assistance at the right time and place. It's this thought process that has allowed me to feel in control of the assistance that I do get and has made it more palatable to receive.

REASSESSING MILESTONE MOMENTS

Having a major traumatic event in my life almost made me feel free to reassess what my life milestones were. Learning that life could change so quickly and change so much gave me a maturity at a young age. Now I have started to process the trauma, I have the benefit of being confident about the importance of enjoying life and taking risks that I don't think I would have been able to do before. I think I have also realized that life does change and that it's okay to change ideas and plans even if others around you might not agree.

Exercise: Reassess your challenges

Write a list of three things that you like doing.

Now write down two things for each activity that might make doing those things difficult.

Write down two things for each activity that you might be able to do to change this.

Exercise: Identify your goals

This exercise is something I used to roll my eyes at, but I've realized it helped me to understand myself and recognize what my most important goals are. The time frame that you use can be flexible, but I've found it's good to have one to help me focus and evaluate my progress. I have also done this exercise with another person and chatted through our ideas.

Buying a goal journal can be useful for this task – there are lots out there to choose from – but you can always just list some basic life goal ideas on a computer. These could include things such as career, financial, personal development, spiritual and relationship goals. Obviously, these are big areas, so I take them one at a time and set myself some smaller goals. This is about thinking in the now – your goal for the next six months to a year – not long term, as it's too overwhelming.

4

ANGER AND BARGAINING
(THE THIRD STAGE OF GRIEF)

'So, what colour is her discharge?' My doctor turned to Alice and waited for an answer. Alice turned to me and said, 'Lu, what colour is your discharge?' I smiled at my lovely sister as she knew that I was capable enough of answering questions about my own body. Alice guided me into the doctors to have a check up on the Microgynon contraceptive pill I had been on since I was around 15 years old. Initially it was never just about contraception for me. My periods always affected my eyesight. Without fail, every month my vagina would bleed and so would the back of my eyes. Like clockwork. And mine and my mum's untested theory of putting me on the pill did help.

Five years later, as I was now blind and didn't need the pill to stabilize my hormones because of my eyes,

Alice and I attended an appointment because the pill was making me feel so low in mood. There was a time when I just took the pill every day because it made my periods lighter. It also meant I felt less sad when I couldn't see my period on the sanitary towel anymore. Now it was time to talk about how it was affecting my brain – and a few other things.

Alice and I are so close. She would run into the bathroom at any point if I needed to ask a question about discharge or periods or what colour everything was. I knew every answer about my body because I made sure that I did, and I felt so taken aback that my own doctor was asking my sister just because I couldn't see. The doctor turned to Alice after I answered and said, 'How are the tablets making her feel?' Alice just repeated the question to me. After the third or fourth time, I felt so dehumanized and angry that I just wanted to storm out of there. It was a common occurrence that people would ask the sighted person I was with for my order in restaurants or when I was purchasing something at a till. It became such a thing that whoever I was with just used to look at the person concerned and say, 'Why don't you ask Lucy?'

I felt angry that the world viewed me differently just because I lost my eyesight through no fault of my own.

Everything I went to do wasn't accessible or there was a hurdle I had to fix in order for me to do anything independently. Nothing felt easy anymore and I felt angry. Often, I would ask myself, 'Why me?'

I was in a state of cognitive dissonance. In my head I felt independent, that changing a few things about my environment made me completely equal and competent. However, society, I found, viewed me very differently. I would find myself talking to very educated people, like my doctor who treated me like a person who didn't know their own mind, didn't have autonomy over their own body and, quite frankly, someone who was 'less than'.

I can't even count the number of times I have been discriminated against. Usually, discrimination is subtle; covert or stealthy discrimination is way more prominent today. However, sometimes it's not so subtle – I have even known of a job advert that eliminated disabled applicants. Denying someone an opportunity because they are disabled, for example; only allowing a disabled journalist to work on disabled stories; not allowing a guide dog user into your establishment because 'dogs are not allowed'; stating that 'you are pretty for a blind person'; stating that films are for sighted people or pointing out that one part of society will never accept you because of something that you cannot control – this is not equality.

Other people's thoughts used to weigh me down so much that the issue was no longer that I was unable to walk out of the front door (I actually became very competent at this with my long white cane or guide dog); the issue now was that I was crippled by society's expectations of me. I couldn't get in a taxi without a refusal. I couldn't watch a movie because there was no audio description. I couldn't go to a new gym with Ollie because there was no unisex disabled changing room. I could not go to a new restaurant spontaneously just in case I was turned away because of my guide dog. It makes you paranoid and on edge. There were some weeks when every day I faced this. I felt trapped in a world in which I believed I could be independent, but I lived in a sighted world not made for me, and people's perceptions of me not being able to work or have a fulfilling life made me want to stay in my house forever – especially when passers-by just drag you across the road. This has happened so many times when I've been out on my own. The worst is when people shout and talk very slowly at me…I can hear you! I have also heard 'your guide dog can smell my dog' about 2,000 times. I love the chat most of the time, but when it's late and I just want to walk home and someone distracts my dog, it is so frustrating.

People's expectations made me so angry that it made me think about how, if I didn't have my cataract operation at that time, maybe I would have more vision now. It made me doubt the decisions I had made in the past because of the reality I was living now. Yes, being blind day to day was hard at the beginning, but the actual practicality of doing everyday tasks now is normal for me. If you did something every day for nearly nine years, no matter what it was, I can almost guarantee that you would be very good at it. I am good at being a blind person because I do it every day.

Most of the time nowadays, other people's perceptions and expectations cause me the most dysphoria about my disability than my disability itself. I think for me that is why anger goes hand in hand with bargaining when I chat about my grief journey.

If you know me well, then you know that I had massive dreams and goals even before my career took off. I don't want to undermine my natural drive and determination with this next statement, but I fought against society's expectations of me so much that I almost compensated by being even more capable and extreme at different things than the average human.

For example, I couldn't just be vegetarian – I had to be vegan. I couldn't just run 5km – I had to run a marathon. I couldn't just learn to do a little bit of make-up by myself without a mirror – I had to do eyeliner and lashes. I couldn't just get a job in my local town where I grew up – I had to move to central London. I know ultimately that going the extra mile – literally – has made me the Lucy I am today. If I didn't make myself feel uncomfortable and scared at times, I would have never grown as a person.

Even though attempting to bargain with myself led me to leap outside my comfort zone, it was all a distraction from the inevitable doom in my mind for a while. I just kept telling myself that it would all be okay when I had run a marathon. It would get better when X or Y happened. One month I was obsessed with skincare, one month I ran the London Marathon, then I became vegan. My brain felt so extreme, and what was happening to me was so extreme, that I needed to put my energy somewhere.

When I finished the marathon back in 2017, I had this sense of achievement that I had never felt before, but a few days later I asked myself: 'Now what?' I would often charge into the next challenge, so much so that I would forget the original rationale for me wanting to do something. Deep down though, I think I felt that, if I was superhuman at many tasks, people wouldn't look at me strangely and talk down to me. People used to see my disability before they saw Lucy, and some still do. Surely if I distracted myself enough and reminded people what I'm good at then they wouldn't see me differently? Well, at least that is what I told myself. It didn't work. I still got refused a lift by a taxi driver who spat at my shoes. I still reported for BBC News and had someone talk to my mum about me in front of me when we were clothes shopping.

I would talk to others about this, and they would very earnestly say 'don't let it get to you'. I can do this more nowadays because I have the skills and mental routines to get through, but when subtle discrimination happens to you every day, you absorb it like a sponge even if you don't mean to. It's like if you told yourself every day that you are ugly. You should never do this because bullying yourself is horrible and you are very lovely, but you would probably start to believe those negative thoughts. If you hear something every day it's hard to block out the monumental force of those actions or words. You would have to be a very, very carefree and, arguably, very unemotional alien-like human not to be affected by everyday things because this is what influences our very existence.

If you can walk to work freely – with no mobility aid or care in the world – hear the birds chirping and sit down at your desk, open your laptop and start your tasks for the day on the local network...that sounds fab, doesn't it? But I can see lots of pain points for me in this scenario. I can walk to work, but I need to check that it's not 22°C outside for my little guide dog Molly's paws not to burn. I need to not only pack my things for the day, but Molly's too. I need to make sure that all my make-up is labelled in order to not look like an utter clown, so FaceTiming Alice is usually on the agenda.

On this particular morning, I order a taxi as I am running low on energy – I had factored the cost of this into my monthly bills. This morning, when I go to get into the cab, the taxi driver refuses to take me and doesn't provide a certificate for his pet allergy... Something that always happens. I hear the chirping birds as I am in a long queue waiting for the operator to pick up the phone so I can report the incident. I am standing in the shade so long that I feel Molly may need another wee so we go back inside as we wait for another cab.

By this time, I am a little late for work so am getting stressed. The second cab decides to take me to work, but, on the way, I have started to answer my emails as I am late. The cab driver hears the voice over on my phone and asks, 'How can you even hear that? It's so fast…you are a super human.' I implode a little because in the stress of getting out of the door I forgot my headphones and am now regretting this, wishing so hard that the taxi driver didn't just hear my phone so I don't have to have the same conversation again. I answer politely the same answer I always do: 'Yes, it is very fast, but I have been listening to it for years and years now. It's like skim reading. I am just skim hearing.' Then this prompts more conversation when I just want to answer my emails. I think the driver says something like, 'How do you feed your dog?' or 'How do you feed yourself?' or even 'Do blind people work?' I answer, 'You are taking me to work right now.' The car goes silent.

We pull up at work and I navigate to the office with Molly. She weaves around crowds as I give her a treat at my office door. I get to my desk and log on to the local network, but the developer decided to do some bug fixes overnight. This means that my screen reader no longer works with my work system and I can't log on.

I phone IT and they come and sort it. The tasks I wanted to start at 9am I am now starting at 11.30am if the technician can even fix the bug at all.

No matter how angry I get or how much I bargain with myself I began to realize that the more situations I found myself in, the more I was just harming my own life getting angry, not anyone else's. Even though I deal with many people's expectations of me every single day I walk out of the door, I can choose to give them the key to my mind or walk by untouched. I will say that some days are worse than others and you should never beat yourself up for feeling these things.

Every day is different, but it is not healthy for you to ask, 'Why me?' every single day. It just made me very depressed. The more I was the victim in my own lifetime, I just found myself in a perpetual cycle of misery. If I kept expecting that people would think a certain way, then I was unhappy from the moment I woke up in the morning. Whereas if I took every moment as it came, often I would get a really lovely taxi driver. I would have days when my computer did work really well for me. I would see lots of lovely people who would treat me equally, know my reasonable adjustments at work and treat me with respect. Every great day I had, the more confidence I got to start to get a little bit less angry. I almost wanted to be angry all the time because that was better in some ways than feeling sad, vulnerable and weak. Over time, I analysed why I feared weakness and I realized that being weak means we know what our true strengths are, and there were so many times in the past when I didn't feel ready to look at my strengths again because I thought I would always feel weak.

If we are liable to break or give way under pressure or find ourselves in a weak spot, isn't it a true strength if we are able to recognize this? We only make our deepest emotional connections with others if we let them see every part of ourselves. Admitting that there is good and bad, happy and sad means that getting through inevitably hard or challenging times is easier when you know yourself and can understand how to navigate your emotions. We can never really control what once was or what has happened, but we can control our emotions. I used to use the word resilience as a weapon against myself: if I wasn't just getting on with things, then it must mean that I couldn't deal with anything, but life is not black and white.

My expectation of myself was very low. It made me feel better in the moment for Ollie or Mum to help me with something if I couldn't access it, but, if they did that set thing for me all the time, it meant that I would never learn how to do it again on my own. In the end, I was harming my independence for instant gratification. Ollie and Mum did tasks as fast as I used to do as a sighted teenager, but I used to tell them to hurry up. I also had to deal with some freedoms being stripped away if I did delegate the tasks.

When I recognized that I couldn't deny I was blind anymore, I became so frustrated that I took it out on close individuals. I felt at one time that my whole personality was just snappy. I recall one rainy evening when I put on my green parka coat with the fluffy hood. There was no part of me that wanted to accept that I had owned it for years and the zip was on its way out because I purchased it when I could see, and I couldn't emotionally let go of any clothes that I had seen. Bless Ollie – he was trying to pull this zip up for me for several minutes. Eventually, the zipper got halfway up, before it got stuck on the lining. And then, for some reason, the zip's teeth split apart, so we were in this scenario where the coat was being held together in the middle just below my boobs, but otherwise it was completely open. I found it hard to feel compassionate because I was just angry at the world.

I think everyone around me was scared to tell me that I shouldn't snap at them because they were so conscious that I wasn't acting like myself, and they wanted to cut me some slack. It went on for months and months though and, in the end, I did need to hear how my anger was affecting everyone I loved. At this point, it was several years after my operation and we had exhausted the list of things we could do to make me happy. I was so thankful that I had people in my life who wanted to keep trying. I was having counselling at this point so I could also chat about how I felt outside of my home. I had just quit university for the second time and, quite frankly, I hated myself. I remember having a really deep chat with Mum about how sad we both were that I felt so angry. I just blamed her and Dad and Alice for wanting to watch films – anything I could possibly say that would blame them; it would just be word vomit. I would make them cry because they felt so guilty, but none of us could help it. Some nights we would hug each other so tightly we would never want to let go after the arguments, but other times I would just storm off. After a while, because I am so close to my family, the things they said started to get through to me. It is okay to be a victim, but I didn't want to be one forever.

If I truly look inwards, I had a victim complex. No matter what I chatted about, I was always the person who had it worse in life, but this is a very unhealthy way to live. It is completely understandable that hard times can bring anger, but after allowing yourself to feel that emotion, always let it go. Because you don't need high blood pressure.

I vividly remember Mum hiring me an English literature tutor not long after I lost my eyesight. I worked for hours after school on my coursework and Mum took the time after work every night to learn about, for example, love in the modern age through literature. She helped me decipher everything from Chaucer to Keats. This involved hours and hours of chatting. She even printed out a timeline and put it all in folders. She drove me across to the other side of Birmingham every week in rush-hour traffic and became my access worker for that time. She bridged the gap between me and new people because she knew my access needs. We had moments of fun when we came out of the lesson and marvelled at how the tutor could make quite heavy boring texts interesting.

Mum was my friend who got me through. She knew I hated everything about Braille and learning to use my computer blind, and she weathered my storm for me when I was my most ill. This meant she also felt the dark moments with me as well. There were times when I was writing my essays and dictating every comma, full stop and exclamation mark when we would both be crying because I would be so frustrated and wanted to write it myself. I hated that I had to wait for her to find the right place in the book because I just wanted to do it myself. I hated that she had to describe the stanza structure, as some poets used how a poem looked visually to portray emotion, and this is what you had to detail in the essay. Every part of me just wanted to glance at it and I blamed Mum, because she was there to blame and was in the firing line.

I feel guilty that we had so many rows, but we say now that, because of this time being so dark and getting through it together, we are so close. All Mum saw was my anger towards myself when I was shouting at her, and this takes a special person. Don't get me wrong, there were moments when it was all too much and one of us would storm into another room. I remember at one time for about two months we would cry every night as we both tried to persist with the same essay.

The most important thing about feeling angry is the ability to look at the anger you felt as if it is outside your body. Reflect on all sides of the situation.

What made you the most frustrated? At what times did you feel certain emotions and for how long? Could you write a stream of consciousness about how you felt in order to analyse where your anger is coming from? You have to remember that anger is not something to be ashamed about. I have to admit, writing this part of my book has made me feel sad to know that I did have a period in my rehabilitation journey when I wasn't a nice human to be around for many months, and I don't feel the most comfortable about writing this down and admitting it to you, but, if I can do it, I know you can too.

DEALING WITH ANGER

Just because your trauma has driven you to be angry, it doesn't mean that anger has to define you.

But Lucy, I hear you ask, if I am so angry with myself all the time, how do I love this new version of myself? The answer is...you don't, for a bit. You are just angry – until, one day, you have broken down piece-by-piece the angry jigsaw that is your trauma. Then you can finally start to see who the new 'you' is.

You have to try to face every feeling that is hurtling towards you at what feels like one million miles per hour. There will be days when you grab the feeling and put it in a drawer because you are too tired and the bad feelings are relentless. There will be days when you want to just be left alone and that is okay too. Let your brain guide you, but know the days when you are able to challenge yourself a little more. You will be able to build your stamina with this the more time that passes.

The most important part of your journey is to not let yourself off the hook for too many days. Give yourself small but achievable goals every week. And by goals I don't mean my bargaining goals where I set out on an outlandish challenge only to not deal with the underlying feeling. These goals for you might be telling yourself that you love the feel of a new dress. Or maybe it's making a goal that you say one positive phrase to yourself a day or do one self-care routine once a day, once a week or bi-weekly.

Recently, one of my dearest friends, Shaaba, came round to my house with her partner Jamie, who is also a very dear and best friend of mine and Ollie's. We were all sitting around my dining table and we were chatting about a comment from someone that really got to me.

Shaaba just turned to me and said, 'But Luce, you are a purple broccoli.'

I didn't really understand where she was coming from with this one. I said, 'Babe, please clarify – I don't understand.'

'No one can tell you that you are a cabbage if you already know in your heart that you are a purple broccoli.'

I am probably paraphrasing a little here, but something in my mind clicked into place in that very moment. If you know so strongly that you are something, then other people's words or actions shouldn't be able to touch your own belief that you will be nothing other than a fabulous purple broccoli. This strength of character definitely takes time to build.

I think the only reason that I was so sure that I was a purple broccoli was because several years earlier, probably five or six years into my blindness, I was beginning to have some self-belief again. I could accept that the words 'Lucy' and 'blind' could live in the same sentence and properly be okay with it. I could be okay sitting with my own thoughts and feelings about life, without wishing I was having a different experience. Just because another human was living the same moment with their eyeballs, didn't mean I was getting any less out of it. It was just a different experience, not an automatically rubbish one.

I began hoping for smiles, memories with loved ones and feeling the sun on my face, not hoping for a cure to my blindness. Hoping every day for something you can't have is utterly exhausting. I was an angry shell of a human.

I remember the day I let myself go on a roller coaster for the first time. I felt physically sick because for my whole life I had told myself that they were bad because my eyesight would get worse. Overriding this thought I had had for 20 years was so weird but oddly satisfying. You know what's best for your body. You know what is best for your own mind. I know you don't recognize every part of your new self yet, but one day soon you will.

Exercise: The anger iceberg

Another friend of mine told me about this exercise and I found it really useful to help understand what provoked my anger, what was beneath that anger, and also how to calm down so that it didn't become too negative, and therefore enable me to eventually make some positive changes. I'm not going to lie, it can be tough, but it's definitely worth having a go at this exercise.

1. Imagine or draw an iceberg and put the words that describe your anger at the top of the iceberg. This is described as the things people would see when you are angry.
2. Now, inside the iceberg, write all the words that would describe the feelings associated with the anger. This is described as all the things you feel when you're angry.

Some things to think about while doing this exercise might be:
- Do you know anyone who manages their anger well?
- If so, what do they do?
- How could exploring your feelings more about anger help you?

Exercise: Challenging negative self-talk
Take one negative word that you have thought about yourself and write this down.

Now write down everything that you have ever felt about yourself that comes to mind when thinking of that negative word. Then you can work on thinking about this list.

Next, take a positive word. Write down everything that you have ever felt about yourself that comes to mind when thinking of that positive word. If you start experiencing negative self-talk, take a moment before gently encouraging yourself to refocus on the positive list and how it made you feel.

I have one aim for you that, one day, after doing these few challenging but simple exercises, you may start to think 'I'm actually not too bad'.

Exercise: The purple broccoli approach

I mentioned purple broccoli and my lovely friend Shaaba earlier (see page 107) – check out her video entitled 'The key to happiness is broccoli' on YouTube which explains it all in more detail. The purple broccoli approach to who I am, and self-acceptance, made so much sense to me, so I hope you find it as helpful as I have. Have fun with this one and celebrate your unique self.

Remember, being a purple broccoli means that no one on this planet can ever make you believe that you are anything other than a purple broccoli because you know it in your heart, and that is the most powerful thing.

5

LONELINESS AND DEPRESSION (THE FOURTH STAGE OF GRIEF)

I think by now you have probably noticed that my journey through grief has been quite textbook. I can definitely relate each stage of grief to periods of time in my life. This fourth stage has been a little different for me. If I place my mind back to 19-year-old Lucy, she was depressed, having a mental breakdown, banging her head on the floor; 23-year-old Lucy and beyond still has waves of depression, but I am able to live alongside it a little more and not let the thoughts completely consume my day, for the most part.

It would be a lie to say that I am completely cured of all my bad thoughts because I don't believe any human is; I am just happy that I can recognize when a storm is coming and can understand how to weather it on my own terms. I never bury feelings anymore when I feel too numb because my heart has healed a lot more now compared with the early days.

Set routines have been crucial: making sure to brush my hair and teeth every morning has been so important to help me stay sane when drowning in emotion. The last thing I wanted to do when I was feeling so low was keep up a routine, but I instinctively knew that I had to try to manage a few simple things. These might seem like nothing, but the process of just waking up, having a shower and trying to listen to a couple of tutorials about make-up on YouTube seemed like something constructive to do. I also enjoyed chatting with Alice about the things I had found out and it made me feel a little more in touch with the real world at a point when I felt like I was in a different reality. The arrival of my guide dog Olga really did mean that I had to have a routine. Her life was full of structure that I had to maintain. I now had another thing that needed to be cared for and I wasn't about to let her down!

I remember the feeling I had when I met Olga for the first time as if it were yesterday. It was 14 February 2014 when she entered my life for good. She was only 19 months old, meaning she was a clever cookie and had got out of guide dog school a little early. (Typically, guide dogs come to be matched with a potential partner anywhere from two years old.) It was a cold but bright day. I was happy, nervous and overwhelmed all at the same time. Only a few weeks earlier, I had had the call to say that I had a potential guide dog match. Bella, my eight-year-old pet dog, sat by my feet and I was waiting for the moment she would bark at the doorbell, and sure enough she did. Part of me didn't want to open the door because this actually meant that I had to start thinking about and taking my mobility seriously.

I fell in love with Olga straight away. Emma, my instructor at the time, brought her to the door to meet me and my family and, quite honestly, I didn't want Olga to leave that day. She was the first bit of hope I had had in over a year. Olga was the most challenging but most rewarding thing to happen to me in those early days. We started training in the February half term break from school. I managed to qualify and learn everything I needed to within those two weeks. It really helped that I was walking routes with Olga that I had recently seen, so the mental maps were still somewhat clear in my mind. I was told that two weeks was very fast for a new owner to qualify, as the lessons included Emma attending my house every morning and training me on all of the commands, foot positions, rules and behaviours I needed to be a successful guide dog handler.

At the end of the training days, you are tested by a regional lead instructor who comes out to test one route while observing. I passed with flying colours, but asked Emma to accompany me on the first day at school with Olga after the break. Emma wanted to talk through with my teachers where Olga could spend break times. Emma drove to my house like she had every morning for the past fortnight. I was ready for her, as I always was, on time. I remember feeling so excited because I had bought a new bag from Topshop that weekend. It was a handbag, so hung on one shoulder. It was bigger than most school bags I had ever had because I needed to fit Olga's things in it as well as my laptop and Braille books. I had a water bowl, blanket, bone and some poop bags, of course. I felt so happy that I could fit it all in as most fashion bags I had come across weren't big enough. I proudly held out my black fake-crocodile leather bag with a small strap and Emma told me that I would struggle walking with a dog and holding that big bag. She asked if I had a backpack. Eighteen-year-old me was dismayed. I did not want to look like a turtle with a huge bag on my back. I was already sticking out like a sore thumb being the girl with the dog at school – I didn't want a backpack too. I reassured Emma that it was all going to be okay.

We set off to school and, halfway there, Olga seemed like she needed to go 'busy, busy, busy' – the three words I say to her when I need her to go to the toilet. I couldn't believe it when she slowed down and then stopped because she needed a poop, even though she had done one just before we went out. I think I hit quite a few low moments when I first became a guide dog user because they are not a pet. You have to keep to all the rules otherwise they will not remember and get more untrained, and eventually may have to be failed as guide dogs. The first six months of any guide dog partnership is so hard, especially when it is your first guide dog and your pet dog is attacking them. Bella eventually accepted Olga after months with specialist trainers, but it was a difficult process.

In the next few weeks, I did replace my school bag with a Vans backpack, but I made sure it was on the longest straps it could be to avoid looking uncool. It really did me a favour to have a backpack because I had my arms free to be able to do the footwork and arm movements Olga needed. I never went back – all my handbags since have been backpacks.

I was starting to get used to a reality that, at 18, I had to wait for a dog to poop before I could go anywhere or do anything. What initially shocked me was how guide dogs have their own little personalities and they are naughty if they want to be. I never thought a guide dog could slip up. It makes sense because all of us have our off days. It took a while to rewire my brain.

When I'm outside with my long white cane, I use it is an object-finding tool. I tap everything to understand what it is by the sound. It is quite tiring for a cane user and most people who use long white canes will tell you that they never go on a walk for fun with the long white cane; you are always going for a purpose. It makes you feel so tired having all that stuff in front of you; you have to be resilient enough to keep bashing things until you understand, but it can give you such a headache.

My new reality was actually okay. I was the only student to have a guide dog at school. The only other guide dog was named Zorro and he was my teacher Ms McClaine's black Lab cross. He had such an unusual name, but he was quite a sweet dog. When you are matched, the Guide Dogs for the Blind Association in the UK make sure your doggie is named before they are given to you. Most of the dogs in the litter are named with each letter of the alphabet unless a company or person fundraises to name a pup. Olga's litter was 'O', meaning her siblings were Ollie, Otto, and so on. Molly is from a 'W' litter, but she was one of the dogs that was sponsored and named by someone else. I didn't get to name her, but it's lovely to think of the love that was sent from other people which collectively did. I remember some of the kids in the visual impairment unit used to feed Zorro baguettes from the canteen at lunchtime, which was quite naughty because guide dogs have all of their food weighed out so they don't get a bad tummy.

Olga's favourite lesson was A level history with Mr Shelton. This is because she tucked into his wooden doorstop for some of the lesson without anyone realizing. I felt so bad initially, but Mr Shelton was so understanding and just took a picture of Olga at the end of the lesson to show his wife.

Olga was a regular in the sixth-form common room and at the end of most days we would set off on our half an hour walk home from school, and she was so good. On the odd day, my nan and grandad would pick us up and Olga would sit up proudly on the back seat, which Grandad loved. No matter how ill and depressed I was, I felt Olga was there. She got me through the day because she needed me and I needed her. I used to sit in bed for hours before I had Olga, but now I couldn't because she needed feeding. I used to not leave the house, but now I did because Olga needed a walk and I could do with a loaf of bread. I felt so low at points that Olga was the only thing that would allow me to know day from night because of her body clock.

Olga and I went to two different universities together, we travelled the country as BBC journalists, she moved into my first rented flat in London with me, she came with me to my first job, and she accompanied me the first time I went on the bus again alone and the first time I went in a taxi again. I had never known a blind reality without her, so I was never looking forward to the day she inevitably had to retire. During the Covid-19 pandemic, like everyone else, Olga and I weren't going out as much and, just like humans, if you don't use a skill for a while you start to lose it. Olga, now eight-and-a-half, was starting to slow down a little early because of the lockdown restrictions and not being on as much public transport or routines with me. Most guide dogs will retire anywhere from around seven to nine years old, though bear in mind that is possibly an overgeneralization on my part because every guide dog partnership is different.

The very moment I knew she was about to retire was when my best friends Beth and Connie came to stay at my house in Milton Keynes for the weekend. It was an extremely sunny day and Olga and I hadn't been out as much. We all set off to the shop to get a few bits to eat, but I could tell Olga just didn't seem herself. Really early on in the journey, she was veering off the path onto the grass, which she had never done before. She was starting not to stop all that well at kerbs and about halfway to Lidl she just completely stopped in her tracks – something she had never ever done before. My heart felt like it was about to stop. Connie guided me back home and Beth went on to get some ice lollies for us to eat. The true seriousness of the situation didn't hit me until the girls left. I went on several walks with Olga after that and she stopped on every one.

I had to make the really heartbreaking decision to retire my girl in October 2020, a good few months before her ninth birthday. I sobbed and sobbed when I made that decision. I sobbed again when my instructor at the time, Mikeala, came over and I had to sign a contract to say Olga was no longer working and she was now not allowed in shops and restaurants. I also had her harness taken away. I shut the door from that visit and cried myself to sleep while hugging Olga on the sofa. It was like my world was falling apart again and, with waiting lists so long for another life-changer, I didn't know when I would have a guide dog again. It could be in two years' time for all I knew. I also felt like I would be cheating on Olga if I got a new companion. I felt so guilty all the time back then. On her retirement date I sobbed as I wrote this message on Instagram accompanied by some really sweet photos. I thought I would include it here because you really do sense the emotional toll it had on me at the time.

This is my gorgeous girl as a young guide dog. In the top picture I had only just met her. She still had her puppy paws! The photo at the bottom is my gorgeous girl now. The time has passed and it feels like the years have really flown by. I love her little grey chin. This girl is more than a dog to me she's my best friend. When I first lost my eyesight she was the thing that got me out of bed on the days I really didn't want to ❤ on the days I felt anxious to leave my front door she was there. Every train journey, every job interview, every taxi ride and every shopping trip she was there. Reminding me that I can be an independent blind woman ❤ we have travelled the country together, made videos about blindness and our life together. Attended a royal wedding, met Zoella and Rod Stewart together. She has got me through some of the worst times imaginable and she never left my side. When I cried she licked the tears off my face when I was happy she wagged her tail and always made me believe that the future is bright ❤ she is my little happy symbol of hope and she always will be forever ❤ it's finally time to officially announce Olga's retirement. I'm not going to lie to you I am crying as I write this post. It seems so real now I am telling you. I don't feel ready for our journey to be over together but it is. My heart is breaking but it's the right thing to do. My gorgeous is now going to have a lot of time cuddling me on the bed and on the sofa! She's also going to spend a lot of time at my mum and dad's house playing with my sister's border collie Otis they are so cute together! Friday will mark the end of our guiding journey. As I look back at everything we achieved together I really am proud of us. I have a lot to thank her for. She has made me the Lucy I am today. At this point, I don't really know what Lucy is without Olga and it will take a lot of adjustment on my part. I'm just really happy my girl can have the rest she deserves. She is definitely getting a lot more carrots!! So here's to my Olga the best guide a girl could ever have. I will always love you ❤

Your relationship with your first guide dog is a bond that will never break. Olga has been with me through times that no other dog will. She was my support when walking into really scary and challenging situations on my own. I grew from a child to a woman and from hating myself to thinking I am okay with her by my side. I will always look back on our chapter and feel heartache, but I am so happy that I had her because some days would have been so much harder without my little fluffy cheeky girl.

I'm glad that I had eight months to work out how I was feeling before guide dog Molly came into my life in July 2021. Speaking to other guide dog owners, it used to be the case that you would retire your guide on the Friday and have a new dog on the Monday. In some ways this means you wouldn't have to battle with the cane so much, but I think there are pros and cons to both. I trained with Olga at home, which was fairly routine at the time though most guide dog owners would have the option of hotel training. Home training became much more routine when I got Molly due to Covid rules being in place. We had five weeks of training and we passed on 19 August 2021. I was so happy that I had my independence back and cried when I was signing the papers. Guide Dogs has been the one charity that has been there for me throughout my sight loss journey. I gave my lovely trainers a hug and our family grew from three to four. I now had two fluffy daughters and I didn't know my heart would have so much room for both of them, but it really did.

The first six months to a year of any partnership is hard, but you have to give it time. I remember when I first qualified with Olga, we met my father-in-law in central Birmingham at the library and there were so many pigeons in the plaza. Olga went to say hi to a few and I was so upset. At the end of the day, dogs are not robots. Even dogs that have over £50,000 worth of training slip up from time to time if they are having a bit of an off day, and that's okay. Also, when you are first with your guide they are still getting used to your tone of voice and how you do things. They are probably wondering why they should listen to you now instead of the guide dog trainers they have been with for months, so it is so important to keep obedience training up at home.

Dogs challenge you every day, but in the best possible way. I used to compare Miss Molly to Olga a lot more in her early training stages. I think this is so natural, as your first partnership is the only thing you have to draw on, but you have to move away from comparison eventually. This gets a lot easier when you get to know your new guide. Each dog is so different and they have a little personality of their own. I am amazed that Molly responds in such a different way to Olga sometimes and I am just getting used to the new positive reinforcement training.

Molly and Olga are wonderful guide dogs and remain beautiful friends to me. They both instinctively know when I am sad and always come over to sit and comfort me when I am feeling emotional. The fact that they both have a simple regular routine is very comforting especially when I am low in mood.

The fact that I love them both so much means that I will always meet their needs. From the morning alarm clocks, to night-time cuddles, with toys and training in between, they help me to get going every day...The fact that Olga's and Molly's body clocks always need food at the same time is at times very annoying when

I want that extra hour in bed though! I have lost track of the times when I have felt them licking my face or wagging their tails so loudly that it wakes me up! Molly has a really sweet little grunt which means, 'Mum, come on, I have really had enough now!'

It was so strange having a dog at what was really very early days after losing my eyesight, and particularly as everything in life seemed so uncertain. I really wasn't sure how to live my new life – everything felt so unpredictable and nothing was certain, not even how I was going to get dressed or wash my clothes! When Olga arrived, it seemed like a little bit of control was starting to come back into my life. The dogs are my certain in this uncertain world.

BUILDING A ROUTINE AND MOOD TRACKING

In the early days, loneliness and isolation were so difficult to manage even though so many people were around me wanting to help. Very slowly, I started to try to build up a routine for myself. For me, it was trying to do some aspect of my make-up which, I am not going to lie, became very challenging at times, but on the good days felt positive for short periods of time. Even if it is just a few things you make sure to do every morning, it makes the world of difference.

Make sure you set your alarm so you are waking up regularly. Try not to sleep in the day and have meals at regular times. Some days will go well, and other days will be a bust! The bad days are not a failure; they are part of life. It's the small steps that I managed to do that psychologically helped to move me slowly but surely in a different direction.

The people around me seemed very annoying at times, but taking a little time to do the exercises below may help you allow those people who care to be part of your journey. They can support you in making your routines fun and consistent.

Exercise: Create a routine chart

A routine chart will help you to focus your mind on the key things that you feel are important. Take some time to think about one or two activities that you feel you would like to complete each day and write them down on a piece of paper or on your Braille note. These can be really simple, and you can come back to this exercise, building up as you feel able – just set some small goals to start with.

Record completion of the tasks daily and make a little note if you were not able to complete the tasks as to why that was and what got in the way.

Exercise: Track your mood

I started to try to think about what affected my routines and realized that negative thoughts and feeling low were key to these. Obviously, I hear you say! But it is useful to make a note of your thoughts and moods so you can track them a little. It can be as detailed or as simple as you like.

Write a list of ten key moods such as happy, sad, frustrated, calm, exhausted, angry or any thought or mood that you feel is relevant. List the days of the week and record which of these chosen moods you feel each day.

You can also write a little about what is going on for you, but just starting to recognize the emotions is useful in itself to help you avoid triggers or activities that don't make you feel good.

Exercise: Healthy lifestyle tips

One of the things that is repeated as a great thing to do when you are low in mood is to exercise and eat well. For me, setting very strict routines or disciplines on myself would often end up making me feel like a failure if I didn't complete the plans I had set myself. Instead, I have decided to think generally about some small things that I can do to feel in control of my health. Try these top tips:

Write a list of your favourite activities. If that's nothing, what's something that you feel you could try to do in order to keep active? Is it a walk to the shop each morning? Is it cleaning one kitchen cupboard each day? Or walking to the post box perhaps? Do you have a close friend who might do an activity once a week with you?

Write a list of your favourite foods. Do you think they are healthy? If they are not, can you reduce the amount of them you eat? Can you add one healthy food with them at each meal?

Can you plan to eat three regular meals each day? Remember, you don't have to be on a diet, struggling to lose weight and constantly focused on this to make a start towards a healthy lifestyle.

6

THE UPWARD TURN: COMMUNICATION AND RELATIONSHIPS (THE FIFTH STAGE OF GRIEF)

Knowing what to say or feel after someone you love has gone through the worst, unimaginable, traumatic event of their life is beyond hard. Maybe you are desperate to help your loved one get back to some sort of new normal. Maybe you are the person who is grieving and you need to hear how the people around you feel from an outsider's perspective. Or maybe you are anticipating a sad event in the future and want to be prepared.

In this chapter, you'll find Q&A sections with my mum, Ollie, sister Alice and dad so you can see how they responded to and dealt with my trauma.

These are words and vulnerable scenarios we have only ever uttered and experienced with each other – from our hearts to yours.

This chapter is hard-hitting, but I promise you it's packed with insight that I hope you will get something out of. What I want you to remember while reading this chapter is that one of the biggest life lessons I have learned is that nothing is simple when it comes to grief and dealing with the intense emotions that come with it; in that moment, it can be suffocating for everyone. You have to work on your relationships every day.

Outside of close relationships, there is also day-to-day communication with the public. I have lost count of the amount of times when online and in real life someone has come up to me and asked if my senses are heightened. Ollie and I were buying a new car recently and the salesman proudly said to me, 'Of course, your senses are heightened, aren't they Luce? I was watching *Daredevil.*' This man did not mean any harm by this comment whatsoever; it was just really misinformed. By all means, please create disabled characters, but there are so many disability consultants out there ready to take your call in order for you to represent the character or scene in a better way; there really is little excuse now not to get it right. These stereotypes are the reason I get comments like, 'How do blind people wipe their bum?', 'How do blind people feed themselves?' and 'Do all blind people marry other blind people?'

Now I am in a good place, I take all of these comments and questions on the chin. I don't blame the individual for asking, I just use it as a moment to educate. I know that it's not my job, just because I am disabled, to be everyone's Google on blindness, but I don't mind. The more people who feel comfortable enough to ask questions, the fewer stereotypes there will be. Anger never works in this situation, especially when 97 per cent of the time the person asking the question is innocent. After I have answered the question, though, I then mention that it is that person's responsibility as an ally to portray disabled people as capable individuals from now on.

The other thing I would say about people's questions and comments is that they do affect my mood if the timing off. For example, maybe when I am partying at my friend's wedding, try not to ask me about the moment I became blind for the first time, as it is quite a happy day. Maybe if you see me tucking into some cake at a restaurant and I am with my family, try not to ask me how I feed my guide dog. If you see me in the street, don't ask me how my guide dog is before asking how my day is going.

I now laugh about all of the examples I have mentioned above, other than the one time when a taxi driver locked me in his car in order to tell me that he needed to finish his prayer before I was allowed to get out because I was disabled and I was a woman who needed looking after. That was super scary.

The moral of the story is that if you are unsure about asking a question and you feel it may be the wrong time to ask, just listen to your gut as you would if you were asking any other question. If you can google it, then go for it and, failing that, I am sure that if you are well-meaning and you have known that person for a while, and you have a very open communication style, you can just ask if they are okay with you asking a question about their disability. Give them the option to choose whether they are in the mood. Our disability is just one part of our life at the end of the day. After all, we are all just big balls of meat wanting to live in harmony.

The final note to say on communication is that it is also important how you respond, whether that's to other people's comments or how you speak to yourself. Maybe if you are feeling like I was – sick and grief-stricken – you won't be able to see the beautiful person standing in front of you wanting to help. You just see a cloud of terror, fear and crippling sadness. You have to work on yourself so you can understand someone else, but you also have to look inwardly and reflect when you feel better. Ollie used to look at me and say, 'I know my Lucy is in there and I'm not giving up on her.'

LUCY'S MUM'S Q&A

Did you ever feel exhausted or tired of fighting for Lucy's rights on her behalf?
The simple answer to this is definitely yes. In the early days, it was almost a relief to be able to focus on a practical solution to something to forget about the distress of watching Lucy go through something that I was powerless to change, a concept that any parent will know is very distressing.

The gradual realization that discrimination is often very subtle and disguised by ill-informed, well-meaning advice was quite a shock. After all, I didn't view Lucy any differently than the sighted daughter I had raised for many years. But, suddenly, I was watching people speak to her differently and make judgements for her, and I realized we had entered a different world. Society's reaction to Lucy's sight loss was not something I had originally considered. It was bad enough coming to terms with what had actually happened, but this was another level and it was almost like I knew I had to find the energy to challenge it in order to ensure that Lucy thrived.

I often felt sad when Lucy told me little bits about some of her friends' experiences and hoped they had advocates too.

As the years have gone on, the taxi refusals, the problems renting a flat with a guide dog, accessibility refusals in restaurants and the people who continually park in disabled spots have become more and more tiresome. I find the range in my response has become more accepting which is a sad reflection of how society and its constant challenges may have affected change. I like to think it's more about picking the important battles!

What are the times that were the hardest and how did you get through them?
It is probably no surprise to say that, when Lucy initially lost her eyesight, it was devastating to see my bright, funny, vivacious, aspiring daughter be

reduced to a shell of her former self sitting in bed eating ice cream!

To be completely honest, at the time Lucy lost her eyesight we had very little support. Lucy will often say that she didn't see any role models out there for her to follow and I certainly felt the same and very isolated. No person ever really asked how I was, how the family were and, in the desire to support Lucy, on reflection, we didn't see this as a priority.

Are you scared?

When Lucy got her guide dog, I was so happy to see her gain some of her independence back. Comforted that her routes had been learned and assessed, I saw Lucy going out as a positive thing. However, fear was never far away from the desire to see an independent Lucy. This could be worrying about cars that could run her over, fear of Lucy's heightened vulnerability as a disabled teenager, fear that she would get lost, fear that Olga would be attacked or fear that Lucy would have issues with working with Olga that would lead to frustration. This fear would often be real. I remember the day when Lucy came back crying after a dog had attacked Olga at the bus stop. We went to the police, but nothing could really be done and it made me feel quite powerless and seemed to highlight the danger out there for Lucy. Sometimes the fear could turn into very real anger and I reflect now on just how insane I must have looked chasing a bus driver down after Lucy had gotten off crying and had explained how rude the driver had been!

How did you deal with those feelings?

Danger is a word often associated with fear and, throughout Lucy's life, I have had to dig deep to bury the fear. The way I see it, we could spend life in a constant feeling of worry, encompassing Lucy in a fluffy white blanket, or we could limit risks as much as possible and carry on. This is true for many of us, but it seemed so for Lucy more than most. To this end, once I had considered the risk of a particular situation, like, for example, Lucy out at a nightclub drinking with her friends, I would close the dangerous thoughts down! I knew she had friends who loved and supported her so that helped. This didn't stop incidents like being chucked out of a bar for walking in a drunk way and not being believed by staff when they were told it's because Lucy's completely blind! But that's another example of how life after sight loss has never been straightforward.

How's your relationship changed with Lucy? What are your top parenting tips?

It's really difficult to think whether my relationship changed from a sighted to blind Lucy as this change happened through such a developmental part of Lucy's life. We have certainly changed, adapted, fought and loved each other over the years! I do think that I remained more constant in Lucy's older teenage life given the fact that she had to adapt to losing her sight. I was always very careful to make sure that this did not become encompassing and, together with Lucy's large circle of friends, this remained a balanced relationship.

My top parenting tip now is to keep a sense of humour! At the stage when Lucy lost her eyesight, it would be to trust in your child's abilities. Ultimately, Lucy had things covered and she just needed some timely support in the right direction.

In all honesty, I am still left working some of this out and don't have the answers to how you manage to support a daughter who has lost her eyesight, but maybe that's the real point! There isn't any other answer than to work at making things seem the best version of life as you go along. I don't think there is a need now to overcompensate; life is to be lived and it's fun even though it is also really hard at times.

Ultimately, Lucy has got this. She needs support at times, but we all do!

Are you close?

Lucy and I have always been extremely close. We always had the same sense of humour and enthusiasm for things, often in a chaotic over-the-top way that would drive our much more considered, loving family mad! We have always been able to chat to anybody about anything for indefinite amounts of time, which can be helpful at times and annoying at others, I am sure!

It's possibly one of the greatest feelings in the world having two daughters who are your friends. I have a similar loving friendship with Alice, Lucy's sister.

Having said that, friendship and parenting don't always go together. Add in supporting your child through a disability and you have a melting pot of conflicting ideas. I have always said that the line between supporting Lucy with a disability and allowing her to develop as a person is a tightrope. I think, as she is now an adult herself, this is easier, but in the darkest days it was difficult and, at times, I felt quite tough and was probably quite firm with Lucy. My expectation of her was never less than of anyone else and was the same as for Alice. On reflection, I am glad of the approach taken, but do reflect on the times when this may have been difficult for Lucy during the initial stage of her sight loss when she was very low. However, this closeness and expectation mean that we never think twice about what might be achievable! We often fall about laughing about how we have done some mad things, like the day we stood and cried in my late parents' greenhouse and ended up deciding to carry ten heavy stone pots through the house to my car as a memento. The audio description from me as we struggled through the house is one to be remembered!

What does independence look like and would you say that you rely on each other?
Watching Lucy develop through her early adult life with her blindness as part of this has been traumatic. There have been so many times I have wanted to 'save' her! It has also, in a very surprising way, allowed me to grow as a person. Her true strength of character and ability to face fears has made me realize that a belief in yourself is a powerful tool, having previously written off people who say, 'You can do anything' or 'You can change things if you want to badly enough' as some sort of unrealistic mantra for the privileged few! I have slowly begun to observe the confidence that has

emerged out of Lucy's life experiences, and watching how she has dealt with them has helped me on a personal level. Now I am not saying that this has been easy. I have observed challenge after challenge from loss of confidence, bad blind days when everything in life is just too much to cope with, physical pain, ableism, constant challenges with accessibility and more. The one thing that has stood out through all of this is that it's the desire to work through problems and the belief that you can that matters. The ability to get to a place where you can challenge what may seem like an absolute unswerving truth takes a depth of character and courage. I am now much closer to doing this after watching Lucy, which I will always remain thankful for.

OLLIE'S Q&A

How did you feel when Lucy lost her eyesight? You were so young – did you have to adjust? What were you thinking when it first happened versus a few months later?

When we found out the operation to save Lucy's sight had failed, I don't have many memories of the next few days after that; I have memories of emotions, but not the events. How does a 16-year-old deal with someone they care about so much going through such a traumatic time? By shutting their own emotions out in my case, becoming the 'rock' as best as I could be. My way of shutting down was to distract myself as much as possible, to lean into my hobbies and try to be as good as I could with them to make up for what I was lacking emotionally as a partner. In retrospect, I have no idea if squishing my emotions was actually helpful to either of us, but I think, without building up that barrier, the subsequent waves of depression – and the anger that accompanied it from Lucy – would have been nearly impossible to get through without having my own personal breakdown.

No one is ever ready for sight loss. For Lucy, she was grief-stricken. For me, I don't know what it was because I wanted her to cope so badly, I wanted to do everything I could to help.

What would your advice be to a partner of someone going through loss or grief?
Listen to them. Try to understand that sometimes someone just needs to vent, they don't always want solutions; unless you are some form of deity or genie, the chances are you cannot solve the cause of their

grief. Sometimes people really do just want to be left alone for a bit. Know that it's okay to step away for a while, especially if the situation is becoming heated. The last thing I would say is that you aren't always going to say the right thing – just know that you are both on the same team, even if you believe in a different path out of the chaos. You both want happiness for the person you care most about.

How do you feel when Lucy is sad? Do you have strategies that you work on together? Are there any routines you've developed as a team?

When Lucy is sad, just like anyone who you love so much, it can be all-consuming. I personally struggle to concentrate knowing that she's upset; I'm not as peppy and not as interested in food. As a partner, I can struggle quite a lot with feeling guilt: 'Why can't I help her? I'm doing so much, I feel drained and yet she's still crying.' Sometimes Lucy's mood can be so 'low' that talking cannot help, so I try to bring her stuff that I know makes her happy, whether it be ice cream, putting on an audiobook or encouraging one of our beautiful dogs to come and give her some love. Other times, I have, in the simplest of terms, a sort of internal guilt where I wish I could have been some sort of eye surgeon looking for solutions rather than someone whose job it is to literally make pretty pictures for movies (or not-so-pretty depending on the project). For the most part, though, we talk. We chat about how Lucy is feeling. Occasionally we know what may have triggered the 'bad blind day', such as a very sighted moment of our life – graduations, for example, which Lucy can't experience to the full extent because the event relies so much on visual images, usually without audio description – so we talk that through. We try to identify what we could do to improve the experience next time and maybe clarify what happened if she was feeling left out. Some days the mind doesn't want to be prodded though, so we try to distract ourselves by talking to a friend/family member or doing an activity which hopefully will make Lucy a bit happier and maybe a bit more open to talking.

How do you think you are perceived as Lucy's carer and what advice would you give to someone who is struggling with who their partner has become?
I personally had never considered that I may be a carer to Lucy until I received a text from the NHS

telling me that I was eligible for a free flu jab. I called up to ask why this was after receiving a few more texts – I thought that maybe I had gotten mixed up with another Oliver in the area and was accidentally taking the jab from someone who could really need it, but no, that wasn't the case. I think one of the strongest reasons that I hadn't considered that I was a carer was because we have always had help from her family. They have significantly helped over the years, especially with organization as that is not something that comes entirely naturally to me outside of the digital realm. Honestly, if you are a partner of someone going through grief, don't be afraid to reach out for help – whether it's from family, friends or even professionals. At the end of the day, we are all only one person and we all have weaknesses, but having someone there to help can fill in those gaps.

Do you look back to what once was?

I definitely think in the first few years, yes. Not necessarily because of Lucy's ability to see, but her ability to feel happy. When we first got together Lucy was super bubbly and outgoing, but when she became blind it took a long time for those elements of her personality to recover. Nowadays, though, I rarely think about the past – at the end of the day, we were only together for two months of our now nine-year-long relationship before Lucy lost her sight. That's an incredibly small percentage. The Lucy I know and the Lucy I proposed to is blind. I didn't pull out a ring along with the hope that there would be a cure. I love blind Lucy.

When your partner doesn't get out of bed, what do you do?

Firstly, talk to them. Why are they not getting out of bed? Is it because of grief? Are they anxious about an event or deadline? Are they out of 'spoons' (see page 201)? Next, find out, if you don't already know, whether they need to be anywhere. From there I cannot offer much more advice as that depends on who your partner is and your relationship with them. I am a man who's living a life that's maybe similar in some way to yours but just happens to have a partner who's written a book. I can say that if Lucy doesn't have any spoons and has no deadlines, I let her sleep to recharge her batteries. If she's depressed and has engagements, I try to gently coax her out of bed with a tea, brekkie and some insistent licking from the dogs. A strong routine can help as well; even better if the person holding your partner accountable is not you – I certainly find I'm too soft and can't tell Lucy 'no' some mornings. At the end of the day, forcing someone out of bed can be emotionally distressing for them, so having someone else cheering them on in the distance can be a good way of easing that pressure. Having someone else put future plans in the diary can also help.

What would you say to anyone trying to undermine your relationship?
I would say that I feel confident in my love for Lucy. That we are a team and that, although Lucy may not be able to do as much physically as me, the emotional depth she can reach is far greater than anything I could even dream of.

What would you say to someone who is struggling to communicate with their partner?
Professional help and medication are not evil. Don't be afraid to seek them and don't be afraid to seek counselling for yourself as well. If you are in a good headspace, you will find it easier to help the person you love.

ALICE'S Q&A

You are both disabled sisters. Do you feel like your disabilities have brought you closer?

I have always felt our disabilities have brought us closer. Especially during the early years and, being autistic, I have always relied on Lucy and continue to look up to her for guidance in life 100 per cent. If I ever had to go to the school office for anything, she would come with me and talk for me; she was always the front man, the warm, bubbly, chatty one. She never made me feel bad for being anxious about talking to people I didn't speak to often; she wouldn't question me, she'd always help. I wasn't as scared of things changing as I know Lucy had done these life events before me and would reassure and help me. When I got to Year 6 in school (Lucy was starting secondary school so it was my first year ever at school without her), I had a panic attack and cried on the way to school every morning because she wasn't there anymore. Part of me felt alone in that I didn't have anyone close to me of my age who I could process it all with – Lucy and I were now going through different journeys when we spent so many years being the same. I struggle to relate to friends who have such distant relationships with their siblings; even if they say they're close, it is a very different dynamic to our sibling relationship. Going to family therapy really helped to rebuild and reconnect after learning about my autism and the early days of navigating Lucy's sight loss.

Is it hard to be sisters to a blind person?
I wouldn't say it is hard to be sisters to a blind person in a practical way. We have our own way of doing things – we have girly chats about make-up, fashion, clothes and pop culture like any other sisters would. But I do wish I had someone in my life who also has a disabled sibling and who realizes my sense of duty and the responsibility I give myself to make sure Lucy is all right. When things are tough, I tend to feel quite isolated from my friends as they're unable to fully understand my situation.

I think it made me grow up a little faster and has definitely made me view life in a very different way than my peers, but I do think that is for the better. Seeing Mum and Dad so deeply upset and affected by Lucy's sight loss was devastating, even more so because they were such strong and supportive parents who always protected us and made sure everything was all right – seeing them unable to fix things like they always did so well was a first. I wished and wished there was something, anything, I could do to make things okay, and I often thought, why Lucy? Why not me?

Although I know she is very independent, we still have a different relationship to other siblings. I will always worry about her more than the average sister. Lucy's sight loss has definitely changed the dynamic from Lucy being my protector to a more balanced sense of us against the world, as we both help each other. We always laugh and say we are a whole person together: I guide Lucy and she speaks for me! When I don't feel like I am able to support Lucy, I feel guilty. I have struggled in the past to put my needs first and I often get swept up in other things as I can get easily distracted. I have realized more and more how important it is for our relationship for me to prioritize my own needs and goals when appropriate. Sometimes I get feelings of guilt if I am unable to cope with something when Lucy manages her sight loss every day but I have to remind myself everyone's feelings are valid and relative to their reality.

At school, how do you feel people treated Lucy and how did you deal with it as a sister?

When Lucy lost her eyesight, I don't feel people at school treated her too differently as she always had a lot of friends with her and the visual impairment unit at our school did help. I remember my classmates were surprised to see Lucy walking around with a cane as they didn't know she was visually impaired and I didn't really talk about it much. It was hard to talk about and for people to be so light-hearted while asking me about Lucy's sight loss – it was a passing curiosity for most people and I felt others failed to see how it had changed not only Lucy's life forever but our whole family's. Other than family members going through it in a similar way to me, I don't ever remember anyone asking if I was all right or how I was coping with everything. I don't feel there was much acknowledgement of that, which I didn't realize was harmful at the time.

Do you miss Lucy having eyesight?

To a certain extent, I do miss Lucy having eyesight, but equally I wouldn't want to change who she is. I feel that there are parts of life we don't get to enjoy together – I'd love for her to see when I change my hair and to hear her opinion of my outfits and make-up.

I especially miss Lucy having eyesight when there are big events like my university graduation and when I'm on stage performing my music – I'd love for Lucy to be able to watch as well as listen. I have always been a massive Nintendo fan – we used to play a lot of *Mario Kart* and *Super Smash Bros.* together. I definitely do miss being able to do that. In some ways, I feel like it's made us stay closer as we have made more of a conscious decision to support each other. It has also encouraged me not to be as self-absorbed with my own concerns and instead be a proper support to not just Lucy but all of my friends and family. The feeling of loss comes around to hurt me at key moments, for example, one Christmas we bought a massive photo frame for my nan with different baby photos of her four grandchildren. It's hard for me to enjoy the photos and reminisce without feeling guilty, and it makes me not want to at all if Lucy isn't able to enjoy them too. I made sure that me and Lucy were out in the kitchen making breakfast while Nan opened the gift as we didn't want to stop her enjoyment. I find Christmas in general has had to change a lot as the present opening can be overwhelming and people often forget to audio-describe their reactions and gifts, which I find hurtful and upsetting when Lucy cannot share in the happiness.

Do you think your relationship has changed because of Lucy's blindness?

I don't feel like mine and Lucy's relationship has changed due to her blindness. It has had to change in practical ways, but in terms of Lucy being my protector and the person I look up to for guidance, it is still 100 per cent the same. I have a pact to always tell Lucy the truth about all sighted things, which can be difficult at times, but it never affects our friendship. I know she would do the same for me if it was the other way around. I always want to protect Lucy and, at times, for example in social situations and travelling around together, this isn't possible without additional sighted help due to my autism, which can be very frustrating. We may not have been as close had Lucy remained sighted because I think going through hard times, and showing up for each other in the way that we have had to in our lives, is what makes bonds between people strong.

How are you now as a family and what is life like?

In terms of how we are now, I think we cope well for the most part. We are all adjusting to things and learning all the time as a family as life goes on and more milestones pass, but I don't feel the loss gets any easier as there are reminders all the time and we live in a very sighted world. Now the initial shock is over, and as a result of how I have seen Lucy being treated, I try to focus my thoughts on changing perceptions on blindness and disability in general, as well as doing our best to help remove harmful stereotypes. Rather than treating sight loss as something that we will be able to overcome, I understand more now that I'll always need to be around to support Lucy in whatever form of support she will need at the time, which I feel siblings should do for each other when they are close regardless of sight loss anyway. I will always thank Lucy for teaching me how to really show up for someone and for also teaching me what true support really is.

LUCY'S DAD'S Q&A

What was Lucy's childhood like from your perspective? Was she a happy girl?
Lucy had a perfectly normal, happy early childhood – able-bodied, largely fit and well. She was, and is, an extremely outgoing, friendly, likeable young lady, always with a large circle of friends and associates who enjoy her company, working and collaborating with her. She has a great relationship with her sister,

who is her polar opposite. Alice is shy, introverted and contained, and has differing interests and a smaller circle of friends, but is extremely close to Lucy.

To preface things here, in early childhood, both Lucy and Alice were treated completely equally. They are only separated by 15 months in age, so, as younger children, they broadly liked the same sorts of things. Of course, having had a routine eye test aged eight, with subsequent specialist appointments at the eye hospital, and genetics tests at the Women's Hospital, we knew Lucy had a degenerative problem with her retinas, but this was seen as a manageable condition with six-monthly consultant appointments at the eye hospital, to monitor any deterioration, with little effect on her visual acuity. In fact, Lucy did not need corrective glasses at all.

As the early part of the century progressed, both Lucy and Alice grew to be happy and well-adjusted young girls doing the usual things, like reading bedtime stories with their mum, attending dance classes at weekends, learning karate with great skill and enthusiasm, enjoying birthdays and Christmas with my ever-present lovely mum and sister, summer holidays with our friends, the Conran family, and learning to ride bicycles on the common near our home in Walsall.

Lucy always says that she ate, breathed and slept tech – and she loved it! Can you tell us about this and what effect this had as Lucy's sight worsened?

Due to my qualifications and career, at home, during the girls' junior school years, we always had the latest computers and technology available. This was always used for homework, recreational creative projects and gaming. As a result, like many children even more so today, Lucy and Alice became extremely expert in the use of many systems (PC, Mac, iPod, iPhone, iPad, etc.). For Lucy, this greatly levelled the playing field in terms of homework and recreational content, as she could pretty much configure things seamlessly to suit her visual acuity. Looking back, I think the use of technology and Lucy's relative expertise masked the deterioration in her eyesight to her and us. To the extent that when she complained of loss of vision in her right eye in the spring of 2007, we were all shocked.

As Lucy's vision started to deteriorate, learning how to use her phone and computer without much useable sight began in earnest. Understandably, initially Lucy was extremely frustrated...as an expert user of phones and various computers, both PC and Mac, she struggled to navigate using the assistive screen-reading features. We had many sessions together, but we found it increasingly difficult to work together. I think, because Lucy was able to take her anger and frustration out on me, this may have helped as an outlet for her anger. But, the result was that I couldn't really help her with the more complex assistive features, particularly, with her Mac and the excellent VoiceOver screen reader. However, I think she did have a good basic grasp, which allowed her to practise in her own time and eventually fly…with just a small amount of technical support and configuration help from time to time, which is pretty much where we are today.

During this time, we were also keen to provide Lucy with some specialist Braille and page scan and reading equipment. Lucy had some Braille lessons for a few years, and this helped her access this equipment. Her school had some shared resources, but with Lucy now studying for A levels without useable sight, we needed to procure some equipment to use at home. To this end, I reached out to a local trust to help us with the cost of the equipment we had been advised she needed. I wrote a heartfelt letter to the trust, as Lucy was hoping to study law at university – and I was determined she would be able to have every chance to achieve this dream.

An excerpt from the letter is included here:

Despite her sight loss, she remains unswervingly positive and totally determined to succeed in her ambition for a notable career in law. To this end, she has restarted her studies in Braille – something she'd paused while studying for her GCSEs – recognizing Braille as *the* essential enabling tool to help continue her studies more effectively with a much-reduced level of vision. Needless to say, she is making astonishing progress in this additional crucial endeavour at school. She just needs some financial help to obtain the necessary Braille equipment and some assistive technology to use at home to aid her in her aspirations toward inevitable academic success and complete personal independence.

I truly believe, whatever Lucy has to overcome in relation to her eyesight and future life, she will be an exceptional barrister, a totally fulfilled, happy and rounded person. Let's face it, with her track record to date, would any rational gambling person bet against her?

Did your parenting style change the more eyesight Lucy lost?

Later in 2007, having been to a local consultant's appointment and had a second opinion from experts at Moorfields Eye Hospital, it was concluded that Lucy had suffered a complete retinal detachment and total loss of sight in her right eye, which was always her better eye, in terms of visual acuity and general eye health up to that point. I will never forget sitting next to an 11-year-old girl and telling her everything will be fine, which was based on the best judgement of the consultants at the time, and completely inaccurate. I look back at that time and feel upset that monumental thing had happened to Lucy and we only discovered it over several months. The full realization was only evident in December, as part of an urgent dash to London, when we were told what they thought looked okay in the summer, was actually permanent, devastating and untreatable sight loss in one eye. With the very real possibility that her other eye would suffer the same fate.

Nobody tells you how to parent a blind child, so I continued to try to protect my daughter in the best way I knew how. I tried to instil key safety messages into her, such as encouraging her to keep a white cane in her backpack, to take care when going out and not use headphones while walking and generally keep a watchful eye. I would always be the keeper of batteries, chargers and the source of the latest tech updates! This was at least something I could do to help in what seemed like a helpless situation at times.

Did you see any change in Lucy the more sight she lost?
Lucy's life-changing sight loss was just devastating. Lucy didn't stop being Lucy, but, in the early days at least, she was more somber, pessimistic and depressed. It was extremely distressing to see her go through this, I just wanted to protect her from the world and take away her pain.

When you got the call updating you about Lucy's operation in London what was going through your mind?
Unfortunately, one day I arrived home from work to be told that Lucy could see the dreaded curtain closing across her vision – the very thing we'd all been dreading for many years. It seems the cataract surgery had destabilized her retina, very sadly causing it to detach. Again, Lucy was rushed to Moorfields Eye Hospital to undergo sight-saving surgery.

This time, it was thought better to keep myself and Alice at home, and Lucy to go for the surgery with my wife and sister…I can't really remember why we made this choice, but it is something I bitterly regret because the experience was much more traumatic for the three of them than we ever expected. From that point to this very minute now, I'd do anything to be able to swap my sight for hers.

How did you adapt as a family to Lucy's blindness?
Post-operatively, Lucy had to keep herself facedown for several weeks. She was also very disappointed about the quality of her remaining eyesight, which was to deteriorate further over the next few weeks, months and years. I must say, this has been the hardest part of Lucy's sight loss…for Lucy and for our family. Heartbreaking, utterly heartbreaking.

As Lucy's sight-saving surgery and subsequent sight loss was unfolding, her sister Alice was struggling with her mental health, with my wife interfacing with the local mental health services for more than a year. Eventually, with Lucy recovering from surgery, Alice had to go into hospital for several months, an extremely difficult situation, with her only being allowed home for one or two days at a time. The family also had to participate in family therapy during her stay. We were extremely lucky to have a bed local to us, and the whole hospital experience was later seen as a great NHS experience overall. Needless to say, Lucy supported her sister admirably while going through unimaginably hard times herself and, looking back at those days, weeks and months, I wonder how she was able to do that.

Seeing Lucy train to be a guide dog handler, and to learn routes to school and other local destinations, was extremely nerve-shredding, as a parent. To think that she would be alone, with a guide dog navigating the world without sight, made us extremely concerned about some of the road crossings along her route to school, and my anxiety about Lucy's general safety and collective family stresses led me to have some weeks away from work with a breakdown and treatment for depression.

Lucy was obviously dealing with her own mental challenges with sight loss and school studies at this same time, but we did collectively press on with our work, learning challenges and building works.

What is life like now several years later? Has Lucy's life turned out the way you had hoped it would when you had her?

Lucy has now moved out of London, has a house and continues to work as a freelance presenter and social media superstar to this day. We are all very proud, worried, annoyed, in awe and astonished by Lucy right up to today, now, this minute.

DEALING WITH RELATIONSHIPS

I know there may be questions that pop up in your own mind after reading these Q&As and I encourage you to write them down.

Challenge yourself to write at least five questions you would ask your loved one. I have left space for you to write these down at the end of the chapter. Don't filter yourself – I want the raw emotion through your questioning. Then, when approaching your loved one, it will be easier to not only ask them with confidence, but also soften the wording depending on how far along in the grieving process they are.

Ollie and Lucy's five tips to a successful relationship having overcome grief and loss:

1. Listen to what the other person is saying, not what you want to hear.
2. Take time for yourself. Remind yourselves of who you are – it's easy for the grief to take over and for you to let go of your hobbies. Allow your mind to relax and refresh; you will be able to handle emotions a lot better.
3. You are both valid. It's easy for a relationship to become one-sided when grief is in the picture. Make sure you still get a chance to talk through your own emotions – everything is relative and, while a work project may seem insignificant in comparison to the cause of the grief, it doesn't stop the fact that it is causing you stress.
4. Find joy in silence. When I was at university, Lucy and I mainly spoke by phone which led to hours upon hours of talking, and the likelihood of one of us saying something to offend one another would drastically increase. Sometimes just being in each other's company without saying a word can be just as beautiful as the silly conversations about Henry VIII's wives at three in the morning.
5. Have friends. One person can't fulfil all of our needs and have all of the same interests, so

having friends can fill in the gaps that you may not provide for. For example, you might be really into sci-fi films and VFX and she might be really into make-up shopping. You are not a failure for not enjoying make-up shopping and she is not a failure for not enjoying sci-fi. They are just different aspects of your personalities and this is what friends are there for. If you always strive for perfection, you will be permanently looking for what is wrong in order to fix it and this will only hurt the person you love.

Now, try thinking about five questions you would ask your loved one.

7

STARTING TO THINK OF MYSELF DIFFERENTLY: CONFIDENCE AND IDENTITY RECONSTRUCTION (THE SIXTH STAGE OF GRIEF)

I remember learning early on, at around the age of seven, in my religious education lessons at school, that Jesus heals a lot of blind people. I think this was the first encounter I had with the concept of blindness and it taught me that blindness was something that needed to be cured. So, growing up, it made me fearful when I learned about my sight loss that I may one day have to be fixed. I know everyone saw it as a miracle that Jesus was healing this man of all his sins, but I was left wondering if I was a sinner because I was losing my eyesight.

Then, when I finally lost all of my vision as a teenager, after attending church for a while with my very religious now ex-boyfriend who told me that he would dump me if I became blind, I became so afraid that I was destined not to have a great future ahead.

Even on TV, a significant proportion of disabled representation is negative. In the 25th James Bond film, *No Time to Die*, there are three villains with facial disfigurements. This links the idea that disability is connected to being evil: think Captain Hook in *Peter Pan*, and Darth Vader. Often when a main character is disabled, they possess a superpower of some sort, such as Daredevil having no vision, but every other sense is magnified or Professor X who is a wheelchair user and telepathic. And, finally, we have 'inspiration porn', a term coined by the late Stella Young: the idea that someone with a disability is inspirational for just getting out of bed. The notion that someone can overcome their disability is so toxic. A really viral example was a meme that pictured a disabled athlete with text saying, 'the only disability in life is a bad attitude'. Another example is two teenagers pictured in prom outfits holding hands – one a wheelchair user and one not. The text reads 'he asked her to prom *even* in her condition. Like and share = respect'.

Did you know that, according to a *Guardian* survey back in 2014, 44 per cent of people said that they would not want to have sex with a physically disabled person? We aren't seen as sexy because we are seen as vulnerable and inspirational. Too innocent. Untouchable. And we are put on a pedestal almost to be admired from afar. When you form an emotional connection with someone you love, you often relate to them a lot. Disabled people are not seen as relatable because our lives seem hard when portrayed in the media. I am not going to lie and say my life hasn't been hard, but so has everyone's in different ways, including yours, lovely reader.

The only representation of disabled people in a relationship in the media is from the film *Me Before You*. Spoiler alert: the main character becomes disabled and falls in love with his carer only to decide that it is ultimately too painful to live anymore. This may be someone's reality, but it is damaging that this is the only real narrative of disability and relationships that is portrayed. I cried at that film because I understood what it's like to be a stranger in your own body all of a sudden, but I felt sad that people out there watching the film, who knew nothing about disability, wouldn't necessarily appreciate the nuance of the main character's very personal decision. They would just read this as: he must feel awful because he is disabled and disability ultimately means unhappiness and doom. Any directors out there reading this, please make your main characters sexy disabled people!

Then don't get me started on my views on *The Undateables* show on Channel 4. I don't know if they meant for the title to be ironic or thought-provoking, but all it does is just ostracize the disabled community, put us in a little box and tell the world that only disabled people can date other disabled people. The line of questioning on the show is most likely to involve how hard it is to live with a disability in order to encourage a cute, inspirational struggle. Interabled couples are a thing...I would love to see a disabled person find love on ITV's *Love Island* or Netflix's *Love Is Blind*. Where are the sexy wheelchair users?!

When I asked Ollie why disabled people aren't seen as sexy, he said: 'Because people are fools! In all honesty, I think it's half and half between the historical perception of disability and the media. In the past, disabled people have been seen as weak and needing help, and have subsequently been ostracized from the wider community. I imagine this perception, along with the disabled community being essentially forced out of sight, didn't provide the majority of society with the ability to open their minds.'

In addition to this, disabled representation in the media up until very recent years has been, for the most part, inspiration porn or sob stories – not exactly a turn-on. So, while we are bombarded with advertising of able-bodied women in tight dresses and able-bodied men with their abs out, the disabled community are left to smile for happy-family fashion at Asda. However, if able-bodied people are exposed (maybe literally) more often to the world of disability, we might just be able to break down that barrier.

Then there's the idea that having a disability makes everyone treat you as 'less than' or give you a pity party. Take Tiny Tim from *A Christmas Carol*. He was a character that was written just to make the audience feel sorry for him for the most part. Other examples include making out that Paralympians are superhuman. This is just wrong. They have trained for years, just like any other professional athlete. Do not undermine their achievements by telling them that they are superhuman. Often the people writing these posts or the directors, journalists or actors playing these parts do not mean to create a negative stereotype, but they do.

As I started to realize that the world wasn't going to see me as anything other than blind Lucy, I began to fight back. After the initial shock and hatred of myself, the start of forming my new identity in the world included recognizing the problems around me and realizing they were not because of me! I began to accept myself for who I was and celebrate diversity. I started to build my self-confidence, immerse myself in what the issues were and follow other advocacy leaders such as Caroline Casey, Stella Young and Haben Girma, who were shouting from the rooftops for equality and social change.

Being kind to yourself can be difficult in the world of social media...but I realized that, if I was going to fight for change, I had to cultivate a relationship with myself that understood that I was going to be criticized. I developed my own armour to bat away negative comments about my eyes looking different or me not looking straight into the camera.

A good few months back now, I decided to post some photos of me smiling and pointing to some not-so-nice comments some keyboard warriors had left on my page. Both were about the way my eyes look in videos. Here are my responses:

Happy Mental Health Awareness Week 💜 This is why you should love your imperfections 💜 As you know, I have been blind for 8 years now but in my right eye it has been 14 years. This is why it doesn't always look the right way when I am filming or taking a photo. I absolutely love that it has a mind of its own. Got to encourage a queen to be independent! Comments like the one in this photo used to really upset me when I was younger because I didn't like myself, I didn't want to be blind but when I came out to myself, I started to believe in the social model of disability and really live by that. I started to challenge my own internalized ableism. Instead of telling myself that it was me who needed to be fixed it was the world around me that needed to change to accommodate me. I read a comment like this now and say to myself that I love my eyes. I love that they don't look or work like everyone else's. I love them so much that I apply makeup around them to highlight how much I love them. They have made me who I am. I will never shut my eyes because my mission on this planet is to make the world more accessible to blind people. I want everyone to see how perfectly imperfect they are because life isn't about perfection. It is about loving what we have and being happy. Please remember that you are amazing and I can feel the rumbles of a changing world. I love you all so much ♥

We are taught from a very young age that eye contact is important. When you look at someone it is a sign you are engaged in what they are saying, that you understand and that you are confident. I think it is important to look at the camera as much as you physically can but when you are blind there has to be a reasonable expectation that I am not always going to get it right every time I film.

I have to rely on muscle memory and technique in order to place my head and eyes in the correct spot each time. This means my brain does work harder to focus on something that isn't in my vision making tracking the camera impossible.

I am really lucky that I had professional media training in order to develop these skills but at the end of the day I can only try my very best to do something that is ultimately a very hard task with total vision loss. I love what I do and personally think that me not looking at the camera all the time makes my content stand out.

I love being in front of the camera. I believe it is something I was born to do. My blindness has enabled me to find my voice and develop other ways to communicate with others letting them know I am really engaged in what they are saying. It has challenged me to be a better communicator and enabled me to connect with you lovely lot. I would be so interested to hear what you guys have to say on this. Hope you are having a lovely day xxxx

Talking to my followers about my thoughts over the years has really helped me block out the negative comments I receive. However, if you are in a bad place right now, just know that there were so many days when negative thoughts consumed my mind and swam around my head. There was a time when I would have never been able to write a response post with confidence. It takes strength and courage to ignore what others say about you.

I took time to protect myself by being kind to me. I surrounded myself with positive people who didn't just placate me but told me the truth about my appearance. I filtered out words on my social media accounts so I didn't have to read them with my screen reader. I also had a different device for my social media accounts that I only used at set times of the day so I could be conscious with my social media time and make time for other things like books and family. I started to build an inner self-confidence as a result of these approaches as I gained perspective.

Comparison to other people has been my downfall in the past, especially with one person. Now, Molly Burke, another blind creator, and I are great friends, but because I wanted a career on social media, I used to look at her posts and think, 'Why can't I be more like her?' It's not a great place to be in because the person you are comparing yourself with is just living their life. They are just having fun and documenting their highlights from the day. But, remember, it is just highlights. Most people do not post about the bad things in their day. They don't tell you about the dog poo they stepped in or the food they don't like.

There is no way you should try to seek validation by looking at others' posts and, if you are doing this, then you have to mute them for your own good. I challenge you to create a feed that you are proud of on your favourite social media.

I would spend self-sabotaging nights listening to a few videos until I started crying. This wasn't about the person I was watching at all. I felt like a failure, but I really wasn't. This is called doomscrolling and what you should be doing instead is *kindness scrolling* – a newly coined term by my lovely bestie Shaaba who has done some PhD research into parasocial relationships. It's harder to kindness scroll because sometimes you want to go back to your old habits, but this will definitely hinder all your mental health progress. Focus on the things you can fill your day with that make you feel happy. And happiness to you may not be what makes someone else feel good. Also, happiness is not achievable all of the time. It goes in waves because we are human. No one is achieving optimal happiness all of the time because no one would know how to be happy if there was no sadness. Find some content that challenges your mind or places it in another realm.

If you have no distraction or content that makes you switch your brain off, then you aren't giving yourself a chance to move on. In order to get to know me better, I am going to chat to you about who I love to watch on YouTube: Bailey Sarian, Squirmy and Grubs, and Eleanor Neale. I love murder mystery and lifestyle bloggers. I can fall asleep to most content on YouTube. I love a good podcast about current affairs or journalism – something that allows me to think about other people's realities. Anyone who makes you feel bad about yourself or makes you question your own path in life needs to get in the bin.

The reason that I started to post on social media was because when I googled 'blind' nothing really came up. There were no real resources for teenagers; no person documenting their life experiences. I started posting on YouTube when I was 18. There have been many times when I have stopped for a while and then carried on, and that is because life got in the way. Ultimately, I told myself that, if I was going to make a career on social media work long term, I needed to learn everything about my craft. I needed to post consistently and block out negative comments.

I remember my family asking why on Earth I wanted to post videos on the internet. They saw me getting worried about comments and views and questioned if it was the right thing to do. I said that I was concerned because I cared. No matter what, I had a steadfast goal that storytelling and social media was my calling. I wanted to open up and be vulnerable because no one else was. I had no blind friends in real life, but when I logged on everyone understood where I was coming from. For a while, the happy moments were the ones on camera because I was getting used to my new normal.

My first video was full of 'ums' and 'buts' and 'so'. Ollie spent ages removing them. We went to Clintons card shop to buy some dotty and ditzy wrapping paper that we stuck to my bedroom wall. It wasn't just any old roll wrap – it was the posh paper sold in sheets, and we thought we were really cool buying premium paper for our set design. I sat on the floor using natural light and a tripod I stole from my dad – which, fun fact, is still my tripod today which he laughs about. I knew I was bad at making videos, but I kept trying until I understood how to do it.

People often ask me what platform they should start on or what video they should create first and my answer always is to go with what you enjoy because you will keep it up for longer that way. Make videos you are proud of on topics you enjoy, and be consistent. The worst critic is not the haters who comment, it is yourself. The hardest things with the best rewards in life are the things I have been scared to do – and social media was one of them. It was the best thing I ever did. I love what I do.

I am not going to lie, but I think, as I have got older (especially now I am firmly in my mid-twenties), I care less about the comments on Instagram. I also think they don't affect me because Instagram has only been around as a popular app while I have been blind. My sighted internet world stopped when I was 17. The internet was all about Facebook and writing on other people's walls, not about seeing everyone from celebs to your neighbour post on their stories. Now, it is easy for me to close an app and ignore it, because a lot of the content is inaccessible to me. When you cannot see other girls posting, then you find a freedom like no other. I physically cannot be affected by images anymore.

The year 2022 was a big one for me. With new management, thriving social media channels, advocacy work coming in and a contract as the new Pantene ambassador, I started to feel that the foundation of a new blind Lucy was emerging. My purpose and goals as the new me had started to cement themselves and it felt good. My trip to the Brilliant Minds conference in Sweden was an exciting event which was going to continue to develop that feeling.

I remember arriving with guide dog Molly, Ollie and my manager, Ange, at my stylist Harriet's house ready to pick an outfit for the upcoming event. I was flying to Stockholm soon and couldn't wait. We knocked on her door and were greeted by her two adorable Italian greyhounds, one named William and the other, a new little puppy, called Beatrix Pawter. Our first bit of conversation moved on to the outfits she had picked for me, as well as how we could work to get my long white cane or Molly's harness wrapped in the same material as each outfit I was wearing. Maybe we needed some crystals or different coloured materials. I announced that my dream was for a designer brand to make a cane or harness in collaboration with me so I could wear it the next time I was on the BRITs' red carpet, after being the first-ever blind woman to walk the carpet in 2022.

I now carry my mobility aids with pride because they double up as an aid and an accessory. I want to reinvent blind stereotypes by wearing Ray-Ban sunglasses rather than big clunky ones that don't suit your face. Having a handbag that matches your cane is very cool – even better if you can fit the cane in the handbag. I no longer want to hide because this is my identity now. I haven't always been like this. For so many years I hated everything that made me different.

The reason I found my style again was because of my sister initially. She opened up so many fashion choices that wouldn't have been accessible to me because so many fashion websites do not have images that have alt text (image descriptions). When I go into stores, none of the labels have Braille on them so I cannot pick my size when I have felt the cut of a top that I like. Then when I navigate to a shop on my own with my guide dog, often there are not many people on the information desk who can help or the desk is behind a load of racks so it is difficult to get to. I think Alice was a big plaster for me over the years. I haven't had to think about my style too much because a mixture of my mum and Alice's tastes always used to match what I would pick anyway.

Alice and I developed a three-make-up-bag system. One bag is for new products – make-up I have received for birthday and Christmas, for example. It will stay in its packaging and, when Alice opens it and I apply it to my face for the first time, it goes into the second bag. I have to apply that product around four times on my own in front of Alice and have it suit me for it to be able to replace something in my main make-up bag that has run out. We then label it if it makes it into that bag. Labelling everything with Alice and Ollie takes hours and they are so patient. I began to love things that made me feel good and were easy to pick out in the morning. For example, all-in-one outfits are so lovely to wear and, because they're all in one, I don't have to match anything.

I used to ask myself all the time why I care if I cannot see; it is about how I feel inside. Pampering myself and surrounding myself with new smells and experiences makes my life richer. Trying new formulas allows me to pick the nicest make-up that feels the best on my skin. What is lovely about having a different perspective is thinking about all of the alternative ways you can think about one product. I love bronzers for the cheeks, as well as in the crease of your eye for a quick simple look. I used to hate using a foundation brush to apply my base, so that led to me using a beauty sponge. It looks a lot smoother and makes me feel like the product is really sinking into my skin. The beauty of it too is that it looks good.

I started to realize that, if we think of beauty in a different way, we are going to get more meaningful marketing campaigns and reach audiences that care about the way they feel when they apply the product, not just the way it looks. That's why I love the messaging so much in my Pantene advert. It is about the way my hair feels. It is relatable to everyone who is having a bad hair day and wants to feel like their hair needs to be silkier. Injecting some silk and moisture into the hair after washing makes you feel so much better.

Authenticity is so important because people want to see real women advertising things that they care about. The reason that disabled people need to be behind and in front of the screen is because input is needed throughout the whole creative process when crafting a meaningful product that caters to everyone. For example, NaviLens now featuring on every Pantene bottle not only helps me as a blind person scan the item with my smartphone and know what I am holding, but it also helps someone who has forgotten their reading glasses and can't quite read the label, or someone who needs to translate the label into a different language if they don't read English.

Designing for all is empowering. You cannot do diversity without disability. When TikTok blew up in August 2020 I honestly couldn't believe it. I had so many ideas on my phone for a series of questions I wanted to answer and knew that it would be really fun to start uploading videos on a new platform. It was in the early days of the pandemic and everyone was at home on their phones. I felt inspired to create because I had a bit of a gap in my freelance journalist work. A few weeks after posting a few times a day, one of my videos called 'How Does A Blind Girl Light A Candle?' started to pick up a lot of views. It amazed me that people were so interested, so I kept uploading more and more.

Then my video 'Blind Girl Does Her Own Make-Up' made it to just under 20 million views and, by December 2020, I was on one million followers on TikTok and it was my full-time career. I felt really emotional because everything online came full circle for me. Around seven years earlier, Ollie and I had uploaded another longer version of a very young and depressed Lucy doing her own make-up on our YouTube channel entitled exactly the same thing and that became viral back then too. It made me feel so proud that starting these new short-form videos was my calling and I had come so far with my sight loss journey and my career.

From then on, I have loved every minute of posting videos and, to this day, I am still documenting every adventure I have online. I am able to employ my lovely Ollie, sister Alice and my mum. I have a lovely management team and I have really big dreams. I feel so lucky that I can work with family because social media can be so inaccessible for my screen reader at times, especially when an update happens – so I am able to create and delegate tasks when needed. My one mission in life is to educate the world that blind people can live normal and fulfilling lives. We don't just survive; we can also thrive. From my trip to Kenya presenting a BBC travel show documentary to consulting behind the scenes at a YouTube summit in Valencia, I love what I do and I am so lucky and privileged that I can bring you along with me.

SELF-ESTEEM AND CONFIDENCE-BUILDING TASKS

Look at the things you are good at – you might think that you are not very good at anything, but it's a fact that we are all good at something. In the early days, it's hard to tell yourself a positive thought, especially when your confidence is low. I can certainly identify with that feeling. I heard a radio interview once that mentioned how talking to yourself, saying bad thoughts, is the same as being bullied, and this has always stuck with me. I started to ask myself: why am I allowing my brain to bully me when I wouldn't let another person do this?

I also realized that to build my self-esteem and confidence I was going to have to be kind to myself. This was a harder thing for me than being kind to others at first. Gradually, I began saying positive things to myself. Initially, a small fact-based point was more palatable to me, but, as my confidence has grown, I am able to receive a compliment with gracious acceptance and tell myself I did that well.

The key to confidence for me was to believe in my uniqueness and stop apologizing for who I was. This included an acceptance of myself – good and bad. I realized I'm not perfect and will never be, but it's what I do with my mistakes and concerns that matters.

Over time, I have purposely confronted my fears, starting with smaller ones – sometimes in a controlled way and other times in a chaotic, upset way! I would be a liar if I said that it's always gone well, but something about having a go and the sense of accomplishment that it brings has been empowering. I have little micro failures every day, but it's how you get up from them that matters.

My various attempts have often been accompanied by well-meaning worried people suggesting that I shouldn't be doing certain things, but it's the sense of self that I have acquired that allows me to challenge those thoughts. This has been tested at times when I am on a train to Manchester not sure what stop I am at, or in a taxi not sure where I am, or sitting in the BBC Radio 1 studio about to make a broadcast with only Blu Tack on my sliders as tactile markings and the quickest of plans as to how I am going to practically manage the broadcast in an inaccessible studio. Perseverance in the face of adversity seems to have become my trademark!

Although I had to have that desire to keep going, I would also like to acknowledge the support of those loved ones around me. Despite their concerns when they realized there's no stopping my journey, they have encouraged me along the way! Do you have things you would like to do and try lovely reader? Hopefully some of the previous exercises and those below will help you to understand yourself, build self-confidence and come up with what might, right now, feel like some wild plans for the future. Don't forget to take small steps at a time – and good luck!

Exercise: Identify your dreams

List five wild plans or dreams.

Exercise: Take a social media break

If you are struggling with negative thoughts, think about deleting the app for a while and shelving your posts. Limit the amount of time you are on social media so you can connect with people outside. Go for a walk and pamper yourself with your favourite face mask.

Exercise: Try kindness scrolling

Have you ever tried kindness scrolling (see page 179)? Give it a go – it feels so positive and makes you remember what's good about social media. Make sure to filter out all of the people you follow on your feed who make you feel bad about yourself. Curate a special list of accounts that make you feel happy.

Exercise: Reflect on your career goals

It's very easy to aspire to things that are suggested to you or seem like fun, but don't forget that things are never really what they seem and others' ideas of what's good for you are not your own.

1. Take some time to think about what the future could look like for you and don't make comparisons.

2. Think about what you enjoy, what skills you have and how they could be combined into a working life. After all, we spend a lot of time working!

8

BATS AREN'T DISABLED: ACCEPTANCE (THE SEVENTH STAGE OF GRIEF)

It was an average workday for me – at 21 years old, I walked into the BBC's New Broadcasting House (NBH) as normal for my day's work as a broadcast assistant. It was 2018 and I opened my laptop to get on with updating the disability section of the BBC News website with new articles from the weekend and to tick off my to-do list of contributors I had to find for the upcoming BBC Ouch! disability talk podcast episode we were recording the following week.

A few hours later, my boss, Damon, walked over to my desk to ask how I was getting on, which was a regular interaction for us. As it was lunchtime, we began having a more general chit-chat about holidays we had been on. I turned to Damon and asked if he enjoyed going abroad as a blind person because I had always thought it is just like sitting in your back garden but hotter. I didn't understand why other blind people spent so much money going away when we can't see where we are. Damon mentioned to me that he went to Iceland and it was a really cool experience as he embraced the culture and cuisines there. He made sure to let me know that of course you can have a great time abroad because there was more to life than just eyesight.

This conversation really stuck in my memory, not only because I felt like I had spoken to someone who was living a life like mine, but it was someone I really looked up to. Growing up, I had no one in my life who I could chat to who was blind like me. Seeing successful disabled people in the workplace allowed me to accept myself in a way I never had before. I could see Damon running a department, holding down a really cool successful job and having a family. This was everything I wanted and I had never chatted to anyone before who was like me. It is important to not only see yourself represented in the media, but at work too. True acceptance comes from normalizing your own reality – knowing that your life is going to be great because there are others out there who are living a normal life having a lovely normal time.

Holding down my very first job at the BBC allowed me to really come out of my shell. Until this point, every time I failed at something I blamed my blindness, but, now that I worked in a fast-paced environment, it wasn't about my blindness anymore, it was about the quality of my work and my ability to output great stories. I filled my mind with how to be a good journalist and routes from NBH to my new flat near the BT Tower. My acceptance story really was one where I went to the big city to find myself. Olga and I frequented the BBC bar quite a few days after work and I met my other colleagues and friends there. We would chat about stories we were pitching to our editors and laugh about shoots we had been on that had just been commissioned.

One morning my fellow 'Extend in Digital News' journalists and I piled into a BBC building to complete a workshop from a disability consultant named Phil Friend. He was so confident in this talk, and the way he made us think about how to portray ourselves as disabled employees in the workplace was fabulous. I remember him stating that the only person who knows exactly what you need to do your job is you.

You need to take responsibility for your own access needs. It is your job to communicate effectively with your boss in order to get exactly what you need. I'm paraphrasing slightly, but Phil really impressed onto me the importance of taking responsibility for my own disability, otherwise other team members won't know what I need from them, and I will spend more time chasing colleagues for accessible documents than just telling them what documents I can read with my screen reader before the work is passed on to me.

I loved that he said that no one owes me anything. No one can be in your mind unless you write a list of reasonable adjustments for staff.

His talk made me feel confident enough to write down everything I needed. Maybe a few years previously I would have been worried what people thought and I would also not really have known what would be best for me because I was trying to learn how to be a good blind person in the first place, but with time comes responsibility to understand what you need from different situations. This has made me feel way more confident to chat to people, because as a blind person you have to work on breaking down that possible stereotype when you meet someone for the first time. True acceptance is knowing when to give yourself a little tough love and when to realize you are struggling and take a break. The only way you are going to find out any of this is to fail and get back up again.

I used to observe other people in my life and think that it was okay if they weren't the best at something because maybe they hadn't learned it or hadn't put the time in. Maybe they weren't aiming to be great at that set thing because they didn't enjoy it, whereas, for me, I always used to tell myself that the reason I was failing was because of my disability. But this just isn't the case all of the time. Analysing why you have failed at something gives you so much more perspective. I am not just blind Lucy; I can also be tired Lucy and not-so-great-at-maths Lucy. I thought I had to excel to make up for the fact that my eyes don't work, when actually I just needed to be myself and work hard and stop overthinking. Everyone is bad at something in life. This made me begin to analyse what the word 'disability' really meant for me. Why am I disabled or disempowered or disarmed by different environments or situations?

Have you ever said that bats or moles are disabled because they have reduced vision which has evolved to meet their needs? No, because that's just the way life is for them. They have adapted to their habitat in a way that allows them to thrive with all of their other senses. Are we as humans disabled because we can't see UV light like owls can or smell as well as dogs? No. Are you disabled because you're not tall enough to reach the top shelf at the supermarket whereas your friend can? No.

The social model of disability states that you are only disabled because the world around you is disabling. The medical model states that you as the disabled person are the thing that needs to be fixed in a world not made for you. I do not agree with the medical model – it has led me down a path where I have just wished for a cure for my blindness and it is not helpful. If every building was made with ramps then wheelchair users would be empowered. Parents or carers with pushchairs would access buildings with no problem. Getting a suitcase around would be no sweat.

I find myself being annoyed that I live in a sighted world, but also thankful that it has made me challenge myself, think outside the box and made me such a great problem-solver. I feel so much more resilient because of everything I face.

If you look back at the amazing famous disabled

inventors that are in our history books, they had a problem that they wanted to solve to make their lives easier, and then those inventions have been useful for everyone, not just the disabled community – a truly universal design.

Ralph Teetor, a blind engineer, invented cruise control. He started to get annoyed that his driver was putting his foot down as he chatted to him and got slower when there was a gap in conversation. Ralph just wanted a smooth ride. Thomas Edison invented over 1,000 things, but most notably the incandescent light bulb, the electrical grid and the gramophone. Edison lost most of his hearing at the age of 12 due to scarlet fever. He found it to be a blessing because he could tune all the distraction out. Who knows, Edison may not have invented the light bulb if he didn't rely so much on his eyesight for his communication.

Pellegrino Turri invented the typewriter for his blind friend who could not write letters with a pen. The audiobook was created by the American Foundation for the Blind and now everyone enjoys listening to their favourite author while in the car or doing the washing up. The electric toothbrush was invented for people with limited mobility in 1954 and now you can't go to the dentist without them being recommended to you. Automatic doors were designed to help people with limited mobility and now we see them in fancy establishments. Alexander Graham Bell created a device named a phonautograph that allowed deaf individuals to see the vibrations of a sound etched into smoked glass. From there he created the telephone. Optical character recognition (OCR) was invented so blind people could read letters with technology and now it is used for archiving thousands of documents and has automated the postal service.

Regardless of whether you are disabled or not, we all rely on something or someone to get by in everyday life because it is easier. Do you really think that Jeff Bezos would be one of the richest men in the world if he didn't rely on other people to help him? No! Everyone has limits and access needs. Elon Musk has autism. This is a strength, not a weakness.

So, how as disabled people can we ration our energy for the better? I have found over the years that my ability to delegate tasks because of my blindness has allowed me to become a better team leader. After all, I am now the director of my own company and have staff members who rely on me for instruction.

Ollie and I recently took a bit of time off work to go to Spain with his family for his sister's 21st birthday.

This made us both feel really old because I first met her when she was 11. We had a good time, but it made me learn how to manage my energy levels in a new environment when I go on another holiday.

This is a post I wrote on Instagram with a bit of added detail that I really wanted to share with you. The picture was of me smiling with a mountain view of Malaga behind me after me, Ollie and Nick, my father-in-law, climbed a steep road.

Most of the time I have the energy to walk up the mountain physically, but no spoons left after the climb that I can appreciate the description of the view with. When I say spoons I mean it is a metaphor describing the amount of mental and or physical energy that someone has available for daily activities and tasks and how it can become limited. Having a disability when you are away on holiday can be challenging. There are so many new things around which is so exciting but also so overwhelming at the same time when you can't see anything. I love holidays that allow me to take my time, go slow and live in the moment with my Ollie. I experience another culture through trying all the different food and drinks, going to the best bars recommended in the area to feel the atmosphere and take in the hustle and bustle. I can truly experience things when we have a little read about where we are going so I can save my spoons for Ollie's beautiful description of a monument and history of a place. I love feeling old ruins and intricate patterns on buildings and spending time on top of the mountains I climb to experience life with my other senses. I don't apologize anymore for getting tired. I used to feel guilty and sad that my disability made me different to everyone else. I can't just randomly go somewhere and be happy I am in a new place if I can't interact with anything around me. When you have a disability it is so important to plan ahead otherwise I am just walking in a straight line for hours up one road not interacting with anything and this can get so disheartening when you have flown for hours to go somewhere. Especially when the moment you stop there is someone that tells you there is no audio-described boat trips. But Ollie always tells me that I need to take all of the time I need. I am so lucky to have a partner that wants to travel the world with me in a different way. Just because its a little different doesn't mean it's a worse experience either. I would argue because Ollie and I think about where we are we have so many amazing chats. One of the days this holiday we spent most of the day giggling like our 17 year old selves after ordering loads of Spanish chocolate to the villa. It is so exciting when you find something you have never tried before. One of the mornings we giggled on our way to the shop feeling all the local plants we don't have in the UK. I was so happy we took the time to do this because I finally felt like I knew a bit about where I was and could imagine it a little in my mind. I have no real visual memory anymore so it is all about the tactile nature of things. Sometimes I fit in so well and just allow life to sweep me away then I neglect my own feelings. It is easy to go along with what other people perceive as enjoyable if that is what they like to do but people always try and fit this square peg into a round hole and it is never going to work. I like that I have the ability to tell people about spoon theory. It has given me insight into myself that I never would have acknowledged a few years ago. Just because I need a day to sit in bed to recharge doesn't mean its personal it is just me and I am not going to apologize for being me anymore. If I physically have no spoons there is no amount of coffee that will get me out of bed after days of getting my brain to work over time to know where I am in a new place.

I hope that when you are reading my words you can find your inner peace with your own strengths and weaknesses. Your biggest strength is knowing your own mind.

RECOGNIZING SELF-ACCEPTANCE

The best thing that has come from self-acceptance has been a sense of freedom I never really experienced before. I do feel failure, but not in the same way, and I believe that it's about learning from the up and down moments in life.

I'm definitely not as scared to fail, though when I am sitting in my living room feeling like I have had a horrible day because everything's gone wrong, I might question my self-acceptance and how strong I feel! In the early days, any failure would have been very difficult – full of self-loathing and self-blame. Now I have learned to be less self-critical and practise kindness when mistakes happen.

It's my strong belief that acceptance is about managing your own needs and believing in your own self-worth. Once I was able to learn to advocate for myself in a variety of situations, it dawned on me that I had an increase in my own self-worth, no longer felt guilty about asking for what I needed and no longer worried about others' approval. I had an increased autonomy and wanted to live my life to the full.

It's not a failure if, when reading this, you start to make comparisons. Don't forget it's taken many years for me to reach this point, and it's a continued choice to accept myself and who I am. Each day I give some time to my thought patterns and every day I learn something about myself.You might want to do these exercises at different points in your life when you feel ready.

Exercise: Identify your strengths

Write down three things you feel are your strengths.

Exercise: Reframe your setbacks

Write down three things you have recovered from.

- What was good about how you managed things?
- What wasn't so good about your recovery?

Exercise: Write a letter of hope to your younger self

Dear Lucy,

I know it is tearing you apart. There is not one word I can utter that will be enough for you to hear right now. What if I promised you that one day words will have colour again, you will feel the sun's warmth and you will shed tears of happiness, not misery? My life right now as 27-year-old Lucy is far from perfect, but what it is is a life that I never would have dreamed of, sitting where you are now.

My one wish is for me to be able to teleport you through time and space in order to save you from all the heartbreak you will experience in the coming years, but it makes you the person I am today. I can finally say I am proud to be me. When you are in the dark clouds you never can imagine a life worth living again. There was one time when I didn't ever want to write a letter of hope because I didn't believe in hope. I almost wrote a very different letter when I didn't feel like life was worth it anymore, but I want to say one thing right now: your mind is so powerful. A few thoughts can spiral into very big ones. Especially because I know you are a worrier Luce.

Moments from the day just replay in your mind as you are about to go to sleep. Rain sounds really help. Even better when they're not just played from your phone and you can hear the beauty of them dripping down the window. Be kind to yourself in the early days. Think about really small parts of life you enjoy because, if you don't even have the little joys of life, you are never going to love the big moments again. This is a message of hope from the future that I really want you to listen to.

Everyone you are comparing yourself to right now does not have a perfect life. You have the right to grieve your loss in your own way. Do not grieve how others expect you to. Feel every feeling…painful or happy. Do not bottle up your feelings. Your difference is your superpower…but not in a Daredevil way. Be kind to yourself. You can't see it yet, but your blindness is a gift. It allows you to see your life in lots more clarity. You don't have as many distractions as other people. When you lose something in your life then time becomes more important. Every second you want to be doing something that you love because you know what it's like to live through a time when you have lost all meaning to life. It gives you more control over your own mind because there is no way you are wasting precious time anymore. When you lose control of your own body and don't recognize who you are anymore, then every other sense seems more important somehow. My one wish is that I documented more so I could see how far I had come with my mental health. Live in the moment and remember every little happy feeling when they are few and far between.

I am so honoured every day that I am a role model to my followers. It makes me feel so emotional that I have turned something so distressing and life-altering into a story that others can seek comfort from. I take my job very seriously and I will never stop fighting until more equality for disabled people is reached. I spoke to a lawyer once and they were so shocked there is not more in our statute and precedent supporting guide dogs. With all the ableism and inequality in the world, I will never stop smiling because I know my little corner of the internet has hope for a really bright future even if, like me, you cannot see the sun. Massive operations and giant brands are starting to support disabled people in a different way. Time has shifted over the past few years, and I am seeing a massive drive towards diversity and inclusion incentives like never before.

Procter & Gamble were the first ones to believe in me as talent and support visually-impaired customers for the first time in a really real way. Huge brands investing in meaningful changes means that little Lucy who has just lost her eyesight will never go through what I did when walking into Boots or Superdrug. Little Lucy will feel included, independent and seen. No more isolation, and it will change the perception around blindness and disability as well as the culture around what it means to be disabled. If more people see that, in our society, everything is made in a way that everyone can access, then small disabled children won't be bullied as much and teachers will have more of an understanding of how to teach someone with a disability so that child doesn't feel left out in class because materials are not enlarged. Doctors and nurses will change their language so they can empower everyone and give every person the autonomy to be asked about their access needs. There will be children who grow up just seeing universal design everywhere because of the work we are doing, and this means the world to me. They will know nothing other than universal packaging and NaviLens codes in the train station. The question will change from 'How does a blind girl pour a glass of water?' to 'How does a blind girl become prime minister of the United Kingdom?' Because anything is possible. Don't get me wrong, it has been hard to be different in a society that wants everyone to be the same. It is tiring not being 'normal' sometimes, but ultimately having happy moments and being okay with the cards you have been dealt is good enough for me because you can make those cards into a winning hand with imagination, daring to dream and rebellious hope.

Love, 27-year-old Lucy x

Just like this letter, lovely reader, I encourage you to write one of your own. You are strong even if you feel sad right now. It is okay to seek professional help if you have nowhere to turn. If you are recognizing that you need to do this, it means that you are stronger than you realize and, if you feel you don't, then that's okay too.

EPILOGUE: HOW DOES A BLIND GIRL...?

As you know, I knew nothing about disability until I became a disabled person myself. It is not your fault that you have questions. I am here to answer any that you may have had while reading my book. Feel free to flip back to this page when you are wondering how to help a blind friend or colleague, want inspiration to think outside the box with your own problems or just want to tell your friends.

How does a blind girl pour a glass of hot water?
Making a cuppa was the first thing on the agenda as a British blind person. I don't know what I would do without my caffeine in the morning. There are a few ways I do this depending on where I am. If I am at home, I just use my one cup kettle. This is what it says

on the tin – a kettle that boils exactly one cup of water straight into your mug. I place the tea bag into the mug with the milk, place the mug underneath the spout and press the button. Squeeze out the bag after the water is in and there we go.

Option two is if I am somewhere else that has an average kettle. I like to use a tray in this situation just in case I spill anything as kettles are slightly more high-risk. I always have my liquid level indicator on me which is a plastic device with metal prongs on that you slide onto the side of a mug and it beeps when you have filled the water high enough. This is obviously a great option as you don't know how full it is if you can't see. It beeps fast when it's full and allows some margin for you to pour the milk in as it beeps faster if it gets even further to the top.

Option three is when I am somewhere and I don't have any equipment with me, and I have to improvise. This is my least favourite, but a girl's got to do what a girl's got to do. I pour cold water into my mug to the exact height I would want the cuppa without milk. I pour that exact amount and no more into the kettle and boil it. Then once boiled I know that it won't overflow because I have measured the water when cold. Add a tea bag and a dash of milk as normal.

How does a blind girl pour cold water?

Most of the time I just use my finger with this one. It could be squash, Diet Coke, milk...It works with lots of things. The other option is to use the liquid level indicator. Just make sure you practise pouring big heavy bottles if you are new to blind pouring. I am probably stating the obvious, but the fuller the bottle the quicker it is coming out when you tip it.

Does a blind person dream?

Every blind person you meet will tell you something different because we all have different eyesight conditions and became blind at different times in our lives. Some may have lots of visual memories left from when they were sighted and some may have been born blind so have no visual memories to draw on. For me personally, I have never dreamed in pictures, not even when I was sighted. This is called aphantasia or mind blindness. You can't picture a scene, object or person even if it is very familiar to you. It is estimated that 1 to 3 per cent of the population has it. My second cousin JJ mentioned that he can't visualize something when someone tells him to visualize it and he is totally sighted – I've never asked him about his dreams though. It does say on Google that a lot of people with mind blindness have trouble with recognizing faces and also may still visualize things in their dreams. Now I am unsure of whether this is a mind blindness thing or an actual blindness thing. I definitely have a lot more nightmares and apparently this is a very blind person thing. I can't remember the last time I had a nice dream. Possibly when I was sighted to be honest, but I rarely dream these days.

Why are you blind?
I lost my eyesight when I was 17 years old due to my rare genetic condition named incontinentia pigmenti (IP) which runs down the female line of my genetics. None of my female relatives are blind, but most have IP.

What can you see as a completely blind person?
I want to explain what I see as a completely blind 27-year-old after having had quite good vision until the age of 17. I could read 12-point font and saw detail for many years. Many blind people may give you slightly different answers depending on what vision they have had before. At the end of the day, this is going to be a description that has been informed from my past vision that I personally could comprehend so it may

differ from a description given by a person who has been blind from birth with total blindness.

My fiancé Ollie has made a graphic from my description of my sight. This is just my personal eye condition, but I constantly see flashing lights in my brain like little fireworks. You know when someone takes a picture of you and uses the flash, you get a little floater that follows your vision that you can't see past for a few minutes? Well, imagine thousands of these that never go away on top of just total darkness. I describe this as totally black. This is in my left eye that has had eye surgery. My retina detached and the surgery didn't work. It almost looks like Pluto in here. I hope the image helps. Most of the time I don't see light. Occasionally, if the light is really bright in a room, I can, but this really hurts my sensitive eyes. I would say in my right eye, that has been blind since I was 11, I see absolutely nothing at all. Not black, not white; just nothingness – like you are trying to see out of your elbow. More generally, most of the blind population can see something. To be registered blind doesn't mean no sight at all. Only around 10 per cent of the blind population actually sees nothing. If I was in a room with ten blind people, I would be the one statistically with the least amount of vision.

This graphic, made by Ollie, shows what someone with full vision sees (the windmill) and what I see.

Can blind people cook?

Yes, there are many blind chefs like Christine Hà who won *MasterChef* in the USA. I am never claiming I would become a chef, but that is just because I really don't enjoy cooking. I am definitely the washer-upper in mine and Ollie's relationship. I like lots of pre-chopped veg and packet mixes just because, this way, I don't have to spend hours labelling everything with Ollie. I like subscription services like HelloFresh. I love my talking microwave and talking induction hob as this is a great way to cook safely. When I have lots of spoons (see page 201), I can use a gas hob, but I do prefer not to. When using the oven, I make sure to add little tactile stickers on the knobs to know what sort of temperature I am turning it to. I have oven gloves that aren't mitts but actual gloves so I can grab dishes with each finger, so I have more mobility. I love slow cookers and easy dishes that I can chuck lots of pre-chopped things in with a jar sauce and we are away. When cooking pasta, I prefer to use the microwave, but if on the hob I just make sure to put cold water in the pan and place the pasta in a metal sieve so I can easily take it out and have pre-drained pasta so I am not pouring really hot water near me. I also have a water boil alert which is a little round flat thing that you place at the bottom of a pan, and it rattles when starting to boil. I use a smart speaker for a timer. Most of the time I am the one doing the washing up though as I have no spoons left by the end of the day. I much prefer to be the person making breakfast.

How does a guide dog work?

I am the navigator and they are the driver. When we are learning a new route, I always need Ollie or a guide dog mobility specialist with me to take me through everything. I use bone conduction headphones and accessible apps such as Microsoft Soundscape. This maps out environments with 3D sound. Guide dogs are taught to learn environments using the straight-line principle: they go straight and stop at kerbs until you tell them to go in other directions with foot positions, harness movement and vocal commands. I can feel Molly's head move so I know when she may be looking at a doorway or be excited to get to a key objective like a door, pedestrian crossing, lift, stairs or bus stop.

I count kerbs to my destination and, if we have been somewhere a lot, then Molly tends to know where she is going. I never walk on harness to the park with her. She goes on many free runs a week, but we go in the car, and we put her free run bells on so she knows to differentiate work and play. After a hard day's work she plays with her sister Olga and we have two toy boxes at our house so dog toys are always a tripping hazard. During the summer, you can find her mostly in her doggy paddling pool in the garden as she loves water and Olga just watches her and drinks out of it. Olga is more of a hose girl.

How do blind people text or use a phone?
I personally use VoiceOver on my iPhone or TalkBack on an Android device. I cannot see the screen at all so this is a voice, similar to Siri, that you can turn on in the settings of every phone, which reads out everything on the screen. This is how I text too. It also reads out emojis, so if you ever send a blind person the poo emoji it will say 'smiling pile of poo'. There are other ways you can magnify and enlarge text for visually impaired people too. There is a tutorial for most of these things on each device, but if you get stuck just ask your assistant to turn on VoiceOver or TalkBack. I just wanted to mention that I feel incredibly lucky that I became blind in a time when I can access technology in the way I do. If I became blind a few years earlier, I would not have had the option to turn on VoiceOver to text my friends back. This is a

piece of universal design that I will forever be thankful for and wish that other companies see what the tech industry is doing for disabled people and follow suit.

How does a blind person watch TV?

The first thing to address – the elephant in the room if you like – is the word 'watch'. Yes, I still use this word and always will. It is not offensive in any way to say this to me. Do not change your vocabulary around me. I watch TV using audio description. It is fabulous. One thing I should mention, though, is that it needs to be on more things. There have been so many times Ollie and I have sat down to have a quiet date night in and the multi-million-dollar budget film we are about to click play on has no audio description. I am just going to be blunt now. This is disgusting. If you have the budget for pretty pictures, you have the budget to get Ryan Gosling to record some audio description. You've got me on my soap box now. In the UK, only 10 per cent of all programming has to be audio-described by law, but most channels have a lot less. I walk in most of the time to Ollie having audio description on without me in the room because he prefers it on just in case he wants to shut his eyes or not look at the screen while he is cooking or allow me to know what's going on if

I happen to walk in the room. It is just something that is our normal now, so it's not annoying; it's just a part of our life.

Do you remember what Ollie or your family look like?
Short answer: no. It is like if you tried to remember a photo that you placed in a drawer nine years ago and hadn't looked at since. It is really hard to refresh that visual memory when you have no memories to refresh it. I think over the years the more I have tried to think about everyone's faces in order to desperately try to remember them, it has made the memory more and more blurry in my mind. For instance, when I saw the *Incredibles 2* a few years into my blindness, when I still had okay visual recollection of things, I remembered the character Dash a lot more vividly than Ollie's face. This did make me upset, and I think it will forever, but it is part of my life.

Do you remember colour?
No, but some blind people do. I much prefer it when someone describes a colour to me now and they talk to me about how that colour makes them feel rather than a description of the colour. Like yellow being happy or blue being cold. I obviously have a concept

of colour because I have seen it before, but I cannot draw on that visual memory anymore. I hope this makes sense.

Are your other senses heightened now you have lost your vision?

No. I just hone in on them more and have had lots of mobility lessons in order to train my other senses, like touch and hearing, to be better than a sighted person's. It's like if you went to language lessons all your life, you would be better than me at languages. I am better at picking up and determining where sounds are because I have worked hard at training with my independent living skills instructors to be better at understanding the world with different senses and making my hearing the more dominant sense I use.

How does a blind person know when to stop wiping? (This is by far the most popular question I receive on social media.)

Let me ask you a question: do you always look at the toilet roll after every wipe? No. There are many things you can do to make sure you are clean so I make sure I do those things. You get used to doing most things when you have been doing them in the dark for over nine years.

Will you ever be a parent?
Yes, one day I hope to be a mum and I am really humbled by the amount of blind parents there are out there. This is a journey that I am planning to document a lot because there are so many people who get angry that I am even considering being a mum because I may not see every playground hazard in front of me.

I think I have always felt slightly apprehensive about big moments in my life happening without me being able to see them, like having a baby with Ollie or my wedding day coming up. Big moments bring out happy and sad emotions, but they always will. I have to see the beauty in that. I plan to document it all through video, but I am in a place now where I can appreciate that I need a voice note of the memories and more time to process big moments so Ollie and my family can properly audio-describe. It has definitely brought me and my family even closer. I also think there is a bond like no other between Ollie and my family because we have all been through sight loss together and we continue to support each other through every moment. The sadness never goes away; it is something that you constantly have to navigate together.

How do you know where things are in your house?
Sometimes I really don't. The reality is that, if I don't put something back in the exact place that it needs to be, I have lost it until someone who is sighted comes along and helps me out. I try to have set places for everything and methods to find things on my own, but I had to accept a long time ago that this is one of my frustrations now.

Do you still leave the lights on at home?
No, because I don't need them to live a completely normal life. The only reason we have a large electricity bill is because of lovely Ollie having to see things.

Do you feel scared when you answer the front door?
I used to for a long time, and I think at the back of my mind I do always wonder what a random knock on the door is. If I am not expecting the person to show up, then my rule is that I just don't answer. I now have a Ring doorbell connected to Ollie's phone so he tells me who is outside even if he isn't in and I am. What is also really good about the doorbell is that it detects

motion at the front door, and it makes a chime sound. This makes me feel comforted that I will always know when someone is walking up my drive.

Do you have trouble sleeping now you can't see light? Is your circadian rhythm off?

Well, everyone has a sleep–wake cycle and my sleeping pattern is very much helped when I have a routine. The dogs will always wake me up at a constant time. Recently, I went to the States and, because San Francisco is eight or so hours behind the UK, I found it really challenging when I came home to adjust back to UK time because I don't think my body was able to regulate itself. I had to take sleeping tablets for a few nights in order to get myself back on track. It only took Ollie a few days, but for me it was a good few weeks. I make sure to have night-time herbal teas to tell my body to wind down and relax. It is also so important when you are unable to regulate your sleeping schedule not to eat at different times. The number of times I have spoken to other blind people who said they want to eat a sandwich at 3am…the struggle is real sometimes.

What is one thing you found out the hard way?

That no matter how hard something is to do yourself,

it is more rewarding to keep trying. It is the harder path, for sure, when you are in the thick of it and every cell in your body is telling you that you are tired – it is just easier for someone to help you, especially if you are learning how to do so many things again after learning everything in a sighted way to start with. But, even if you are a bit slower than you used to be, it is better to keep trying and trying.

How does a blind person go up and down the stairs?
I used to feel scared about walking down stairs as it felt like it was impending doom and I was going to plunge to my death. Mum used to tell me it was the one thing she used to worry about me doing in the early days, but it is very simple now. At home I use no mobility aid and I just know how many steps there are by feeling with my feet. If I am in a new environment, I use my long white cane to navigate to the steps. I hold the cane out in front of me on the step below, which I am about to walk down, and tap each step before I walk on it. It is really easy to feel when you are coming up to the bottom step. Going up is even easier with a cane as you just tap until it flattens. Guide dogs are also taught to find stairs as a 'key objective' during their training.

How does a blind person light a candle?

I love candles that are smelly and ones that make a crackling sound when they are lit so it makes you feel like you are next to a fire. I love feeling the heat on my skin when it is lit. Obviously this is something that I have to be careful about, but I use a long lighter and make sure to only click the lighter on when I have made sure that it is near the wick. It is easier for me to have candles with several wicks because they light more easily. I also use matches, but I make sure the candle is on a glass table if I do so, as it's not flammable.

How do you read letters?

I have lots of apps that scan all of the text that comes through the door. Ollie also helps me because it can be overwhelming sometimes.

Can you do everything around the house?

I can do a lot of things, but it really does depend on my energy levels. I ration my energy and make sure to delegate tasks. For example, I have a cleaner. The amount of energy that it would take me to do a deep clean of my house when I am working more than full-time and running a business, would just be unachievable. I love that my blindness has allowed me to not feel guilty about accepting help.

Why do blind people have white sticks?

Blind people have used sticks and canes as mobility aids for centuries, but in 1921 a photographer from Bristol named James Biggs painted his white to be more visible. From then, in 1930 the state of Illinois in the USA granted extra protections and right of way to blind people with white canes. Then, in 1931, Guilly d'Herbemont launched a national white stick movement in France for blind citizens and WWI veterans, leading to thousands of white cane users. In 1944, Richard Hoover refined the design of the cane and developed the standard method of long white cane training, named step training. He is referred to as the 'father of the lightweight long cane technique'.

Why do some individuals have red stripes on their cane?

In the UK, this is a symbol that you are registered deaf blind; however, in the States I know that registered blind individuals also have red and white canes. Each country seems to have its own standardized system.

How does a blind person know what's in a jar?
Most of the time I smell what is in there. This is why I get so annoyed when I have a cold and I lose my sense of smell. It really makes me realize how much I rely on it as a blind person. I also label jars in different ways. One way is with Braille labels. Another is using my PenFriend labeller, which is a device that comes with stickers and you can record little voice notes on the stickers and, whenever you hover the pen over the sticker, it plays the last thing you recorded, so it's a great way of knowing what is in the jar after going over what it is with a sighted person. The only trouble comes when your pen runs out of battery!

Do blind people blink?
Yes, unless they have been in a traumatic incident that makes them not able to. At the end of the day, our eyelids have muscles that control them. If you have been blind from birth, there is less of a need to open and close your eyes, but your eyelids are still used to keep your eyes clean, so most blind people blink in order to lubricate the eye otherwise they would have dry eyes. If you don't use your eyelids, then the muscles may atrophy, so keep blinking!

ACKNOWLEDGEMENTS

Where do I start...? My eyes gave up on me that one day, but these gorgeous individuals never did, and I wanted to say, thanks to the beautiful humans who made this book possible.

Mum and Dad, thank you for giving me the strength to tell my story, so other little Lucys out there never go through what I did when I lost my eyesight. You never let me believe that I was anything other than strong independent Lucy.

For you my dearest sister Alice, my best friend. Here's to all those times you loved me enough to describe hours of beauty videos that would have otherwise been inaccessible to me. You have taught me how to be patient and to never give up. With you I can feel myself again.

And my beautiful Ollie. You tape up my wings when I don't want to fly anymore. You are my rock when everything gets tough and I'm so lucky. I share this life with you. Thank you for sitting with me and correcting my many ramblings to share with the world. With you, this life is exciting and limitless.

Auntie Kaz, thank you for believing in me when I didn't believe in myself. Thank you for telling me this would not be the end of Lucy Edwards when sitting beside my hospital bed that day. My lovely second mum, my nutter!

Connie and Beth, my beautiful best friends. Thank you for being there for me. All those lovely walks in the park with the doggies. We are so lucky to have each other and I know we've been friends for more than ten years but I can't wait for ten more! Hopefully we can get old and eat scones together while reading all of the many books that I will have published piled up on your bookshelves!

Thank you to my beautiful retired guide dog, Olga, and to my cheeky guide dog, Miss Molly. You girls are my eyes and my independence. My light in this darkness. Molly, thank you for guiding me to the shop to get some much-needed chocolate during this process.

Thank you to all the people that follow my story online and watch the many reports and documentaries I present on the BBC. Without your support I don't know what I would do. I hope this book helps you get through tough times and makes you smile. Remember there is always sunshine after the storm.

ACKNOWLEDGEMENTS

Thank you to the Bell Lomax Team and the Spotlight Management Team for helping to make this book possible.

And finally, thank you so much to the whole team at Octopus Publishing Group for giving me this opportunity to share my story with the world. Eleanor, I will never forget that you believed in me.

ENDNOTES

Chapter 7

Did you know that according to a Guardian survey...
Mann, Jim, "British sex survey 2014: 'the nation has lost some
of its sexual swagger'", the *Guardian*, www.theguardian.com/
lifeandstyle/2014/sep/28/british-sexsurvey-2014-nation-lost-sexual-
swagger, 28 September 2014 (accessed November 2022).